WINERIES
OF THE FINGER LAKES REGION

The Heart of New York State

Emerson Klees

Friends of the Finger Lakes Publishing
Rochester, New York (www.fingerlakes.com)

Other books about New York State by Emerson Klees

Persons, Places, and Things In the Finger Lakes Region
   (1993, 2000)
Person, Places, and Things Around the Finger Lakes Region
   (1994)
People of the Finger Lakes Region (1995)
Legends and Stories of the Finger Lakes Region (1995)
The Erie Canal in the Finger Lakes Region (1996)
Underground Railroad Tales With Routes Through the
   Finger Lakes Region (1997)
More Legends and Stories of the Finger Lakes Region (1997)
The Women's Rights Movement and the Finger Lakes
   Region (1998)
The Crucible of Ferment: New York's Psychic Highway
   (2001)
The Iroquois Confederacy: History and Legends (2003)

Copyright © 2000, 2003 by Emerson C. Klees

Friends of the Finger Lakes Publishing
P. O. Box 18131
Rochester, New York 14618

Library of Congress Control Number 00-091108

ISBN 1-891046-03-9

Printed in the United States of America
9 8 7 6 5 4 3 2

PREFACE

Wineries of the Finger Lakes Region: The Heart of New York State highlights over 70 wineries in the Finger Lakes Region. This heart-shaped area is bounded by Route 390 in the West, the New York State Thruway in the North, Route 81 Expressway and Route 13 in the East, and the Southern Tier Expressway (Route 17 / I-86) in the South.

The Finger Lakes Region, an area of scenic lake-country beauty, provides diverse vacation opportunities in a region comprised of 14 counties, 264 municipalities, and over 9,000 square miles. Sites and activities in the region include parks, forests, and trails; shows and festivals; lake cruises and boating; waterfalls; museums; historic sites; and fishing and water sports, in addition to wineries.

The number of wineries in the Finger Lakes Region has grown from 19 in 1975 to over 70 in 2003. Visits to regional wineries have increased from 700,000 in the mid-1970s to 2.8 million in 2001. Wineries have become the top-ranked tourist destination in the Finger Lakes Region.

Wineries of the Finger Lakes Region: The Heart of New York State provides an overview of the wineries, including the grapes that they grow and the wine that they make, along with a brief history of winemaking in the region and a description of grape varieties. A glossary of grape and wine terms is provided as well as biographical sketches of some of the area's winemaking pioneers. Showcasing the Finger Lakes Wine Region is discussed in the epilogue. Some of the material in this book is reprinted from *Persons, Places, and Things In the Finger Lakes Region.*

LIST OF PHOTOGRAPHS

Front cover: Courtesy John N. Holtman, Fairport, NY.
Back cover: Courtesy Dr. Frank's Vinifera Wine Cellars

Photographs were provided by the New York Wine & Grape Foundation and Finger Lakes Tourism, Penn Yan, NY.

Cover design by Dunn and Rice Design, Inc. Rochester, NY.

Maps by Actionmaps, Rochester, NY.

The [vector art] images used herein were obtained from IMSI's MasterClips Collection, 1895 Francisco Blvd. East, San Rafael, CA 94901-5506, USA.

TABLE OF CONTENTS

WINERIES OF THE FINGER LAKES REGION

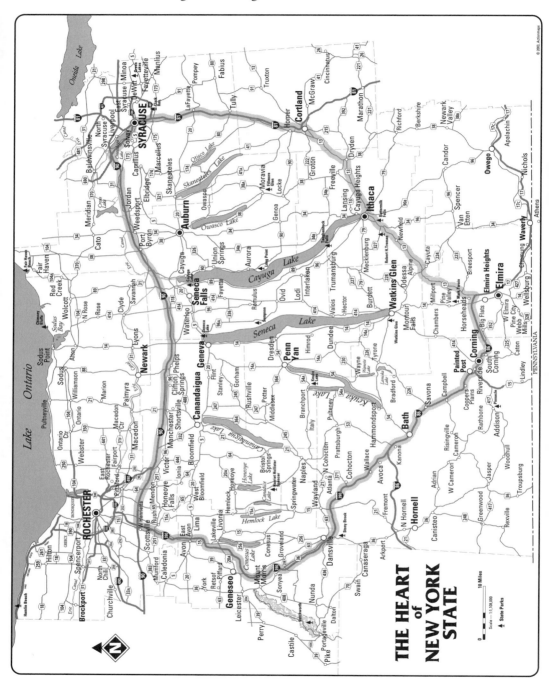

THE HEART
of
NEW YORK STATE

PROLOGUE

History of Winemaking in the Eastern U.S.

"The Eastern United States, with its largely untapped potential for wine production, is a new frontier for American wine much as the West once was for American pioneers. Establishing a vineyard and winery east of the Rockies has many parallels with homesteading in the Old West: developing a modus operandi in a new environment, aiming to transform dreams into realities....

An advantage of winegrowing in the East is that the climate produces fresh-tasting wines, with higher acidity and lower alcoholic content than most from California, the largest wine-producing state....

If variety is the spice of life, the most flavorful wine region of all lies east of the Rockies. The East's many climates and cornucopia of grape varieties provide an exciting challenge for wine adventurers—whether the adventure is producing one's own wine or enjoying new experiences in wine tasting."

Lucie T. Morton in *Winegrowing in Eastern America*

In 1694, Governor William Penn established a vineyard on the east bank of the Schuylkill River in Philadelphia in which he attempted to grow *Vitis vinifera* (European) grapes. Vine pests and diseases caused his experiment to fail. Pollen from this vineyard was carried to a wild *Vitis labrusca* vine to create the red Alexander grape, also known as Cape and Black Cape.

Around 1740, John Alexander, gardener of Lieutenant Governor John Penn, found a grapevine growing along the Schuylkill River and transplanted it to Penn's garden. The Alexander grape was more winter hardy and disease resistant than the *Vitis vinifera* varieties planted earlier. In 1793, Pierre Legaux established the Pennsylvania Wine Company at his Spring Mill vineyard and became the first commercial vineyardist in the United States. His principal grape was the Alexander.

Thomas Jefferson tried unsuccessfully over a period of many years to establish a wine industry in Virginia. He had developed an interest in wine during his years as Minister to France. He gave 2,000 acres adjacent to Monticello to Philip Mazzei, a vineyardist from Italy. In 1773, Mazzei brought thousands of *Vitis vinifera* vines from Tuscany along with trained vineyardists to plant and care for them. However, the Revolutionary War shifted priority from his vineyard project.

In 1809, Jefferson wrote a letter to grapegrowing pioneer John Adlum:

> Sir:
> While I lived in Washington, a member of Congress from your state presented me with ... wine made by you; a dark red wine made from a wild or native grape, called in Maryland the Fox grape, but was very different from what is called by that name in Virginia. This was a very fine wine, and so exactly resembling the red Burgundy of Chambertin that on fair com-

parison with that, of which I had very good on the same table imported by myself from the place where made, the company could not distinguish one from the other. I think that it would be well to push the culture of that grape without losing our time and efforts in search of foreign vines, which it will take centuries to adapt to our soil and climate.

Adlum replied to Jefferson that the wine that was similar to Chambertin was made from Alexander grapes, a *Vitis vinifera-Vitis labrusca* hybrid. Alexander was the first variety to move out of the hedgerows and onto trellises in cultivated vineyards.

Jefferson's advice was taken. The first vineyards in Ohio, Pennsylvania, and Indiana were planted with Alexander grapevines during the early 1800s. In 1818, the first commercial vineyards for wine grapes were planted by Thomas Eichelberger in York, Pennsylvania, near the Susquehanna River.

During the next 50 years, the Alexander grape was overshadowed by improved varieties such as Isabella, introduced by William Prince of Flushing, New York, in 1816; Catawba by John Adlum of Washington, D.C., in 1823; Concord by Ephram Bull of Concord, Massachusetts, in 1852; and Elvira by Jacob Rommel of Missouri in 1870.

In 1825, Nicholas Longworth, a Cincinnati lawyer, purchased Catawba vines from John Adlum and planted vineyards along the Ohio River. Longworth's sparkling Catawba was the first sparkling wine made in the United States. Ohio became the leading wine-producing state during the 1850s. Catawba was the favorite wine grape except in the South, where Scuppernong was preferred.

By the 1860s, Longworth's Catawba vineyards along the Ohio River were struggling. Diseases that had destroyed the early *Vitis vinifera* vineyards were attacking Catawba vines planted in the warm climate of southern Ohio. Powdery mildew, which thrives in hot, dry conditions; downy mildew that favors cool, moist climates; and black rot, which prospers in warm, humid conditions, decimated Catawba plantings as it had *Vitis vinifera* vineyards earlier.

Sulfur was effective against powdery mildew but was ineffective against downy mildew and black rot. Bordeaux mixture, a combination of copper sulfate, lime, and water was developed to control downy mildew and black rot in 1885 — too late to save the vineyards in southern Ohio. Ohio's grape-growing region shifted to the cooler climate of northern Ohio along Lake Erie. In the 1860s, Missouri became the leading grower of wine grapes.

In the mid-1800s, a viticultural disaster occurred. Native-American vine cuttings had been sent to Europe for experimentation and hybridization with *Vitis vinifera* varieties. The aphid Phylloxera accompanied the vine cuttings to Europe. Vines in old, established vineyards began to die for unknown reasons. The French government funded research to try to save the country's six million acres of vineyards.

Research showed that if vineyardists grafted *Vitis vinifera* vines onto disease-resistant rootstock, European varieties could survive against the Phylloxera. Native rootstocks selected for grafting included Couderc 3309, a hybrid of *Vitis riparia* and *Vitis rupestris*; and SO_4 and 5BB, hybrids of *Vitis riparia* and *Vitis berlandieri*, which is native to Texas.

Grafting helped the French wine industry to survive but increased the cost of making wine. Although the industry recovered, acreage of wine grapes decreased from six million acres to three million acres in France. Although grafting was effective against Phylloxera, it did not provide protection against vine diseases such as powdery mildew, downy mildew, and black rot.

Hermann Jaeger of Missouri and T. V. Munson of Texas sent cuttings to France to aid the Europeans in developing Phylloxera-resistant rootstocks and *Vitis vinifera-Vitis labrus-*

ca hybrids. In 1888, Jaeger and Munson were awarded the French Legion of Honor in appreciation of their help during the Phylloxera crisis. Munson is the author of *Foundations of American Grape Culture*.

Grapegrowing in New York State developed in three regions: the Finger Lakes Region, the Hudson River Valley, and the Chautauqua Region along Lake Erie. In 1829 in the rectory garden of St. James Episcopal Church in Hammondsport, Reverend William Bostwick planted the first grapevines in the Finger Lakes Region, Catawba and Isabella vines from the Hudson River Valley.

In 1839, Blooming Grove Winery was established by Jean Jacques in Washingtonville to make altar wines. This Hudson River Valley winery, called Brotherhood Winery today, is the oldest active winery in the United States.

The Chautauqua Region became the largest grapegrowing region in the State by focusing on growing *Vitis labrusca* varieties, such as Concord, for grape juice. The area along Lake Erie became the principal supplier of grapes to Welch's.

The Concord grape variety was introduced in Concord, Massachusetts, in 1852. Horace Greeley said that Concord was "the grape for the millions." In 1866, Concord was awarded the Greeley prize as the best all-around grape variety. It is an adaptable and disease-resistant grape that is productive and easy to grow. However, its foxy or grapey taste prevented it from becoming an acceptable wine grape. Better wine could be made from Cynthiana and Norton varieties, but they were not as easy to grow or as hardy as Concord.

Late in the 19th century, the temperance movement gained momentum. Carrie Nation was in the news, chopping up bars with her hatchet. In the 1870s, Prohibitionist dentist Dr. Thomas Welch's grape juice ("unfermented wine") gained popularity. Grapegrowers were willing to plant additional acres of Concord instead of more difficult-to-grow wine grapes.

The most popular wine in the years prior to the beginning

of Prohibition in 1919 was Virginia Dare, a blend of Scuppernong, Concord, and California *Vitis vinifera*. The taste of Scuppernong dominated, despite the strong taste of Concord. North Carolina grapegrower Paul Garrett, with wineries in six states, became a multi-millionaire making wine for the U.S. market.

The temperance movement gained momentum slowly, beginning with the 1816 law banning the sale of alcoholic beverages on Sunday. During the 1840s, many towns and counties in the East and Midwest went dry. Entire states began to go dry, beginning with Kansas in 1880 and Iowa in 1882. On January 16, 1919, the 18th Amendment (the Prohibition Amendment) to the Constitution was ratified.

Unfortunately, wine was grouped with hard liquor as "intoxicating" by the Volstead Act that became law on October 28, 1919. President Wilson had proposed defining as "intoxicating" drinks containing more than 10 to 12 percent alcohol. The wine industry would have been saved; however, Wilson's veto was overridden by Congress.

Most wineries went out of business. Some tried to stay profitable by producing medicinal and sacramental wines for a very small market. On December 5, 1933, the 21st Amendment to the Constitution was ratified, repealing Prohibition. Three individuals contributed heavily in helping the U.S. wine industry recover from Prohibition: Frank Schoonmaker of New York City, Philip Wagner of Maryland, and Leon Adams of California.

Schoonmaker was a wine importer and author of the *Complete Wine Book* (1934) and *American Wines* (1941). Although he was an importer of European wines, he was optimistic about grapegrowing and winemaking in the United States. By emphasizing the selection of the appropriate grape varieties for each growing region, he correctly identified one of the early shortcomings of growing wine grapes in America. He advocated varietal labeling instead of relying exclusively on blends.

Schoonmaker was not a wine snob; he could appreciate some of the *Vitis labrusca* varieties while recognizing the shortcomings of others:

> In good years, the wine made from the unblended juice of Elvira grapes, grown in the Finger Lakes Region, is exceeded by none produced in the East. Pale straw in color, it has a delightful fragrance, recalling that of a young Moselle, with enough of the native American character to give it individuality. Its acidity is high; a factor which contributes to the refreshing quality of the wine....

> As a true wine grape, it [Concord] has almost nothing to recommend it; it can hardly be made into wine at all unless heavily sugared, and a dry Concord table wine is assertive in flavor and extremely common.

Philip Wagner, editor of the Baltimore *Sun*, went beyond wine appreciation; he became a grapegrower, an amateur winemaker, and author of *American Wines and How to Make Them* (1933) and *A Wine-Growers Guide* (1973). Wagner realized that growing *Vitis vinifera* grapes in his Maryland vineyard would be difficult. He read French grapegrowing literature and discovered hybrids of American and European wine varieties developed in France. He visited France in 1936-37 and found that these hybrids were being used principally as wine grapes and that some of them had been sent to vineyardists in the United States.

In 1942, Wagner and his wife, Jocelyn, established a commercial nursery to provide French-American hybrid vines to U.S. grapegrowers. In 1945, Wagner established a bonded winery, Boordy Vineyards, to produce wine from French-American hybrid grapes.

Leon Adams, journalist, wine historian, and wine pioneer, advocated drinking wine in moderation. In 1931, he founded the California Grape Growers League that preceded the establishment of the Wine Institute in 1934 and the Wine Advisory Board in 1938. Board money financed grape research at universities, establishment of wine quality standards, and lobbyists to work with state governments, the federal government, and international wine organizations.

In 1942, Adams wrote *The Wine Study Course,* followed by the *Commonsense Book of Wine* in 1958 and the *Commonsense Book of Drinking* in 1960. In 1973, he wrote his classic book, *The Wines of America.* Adams traveled around the country as well as Canada and Mexico for 20 years gathering material for this book. Wearing his signature bow tie and usually puffing on a pipe, he visited wineries to inquire about their new developments in grapegrowing and winemaking.

Adams urged grapegrowers to work with their state legislators and departments of agriculture to allow wineries at their vineyards. He believed that "agriculture can defeat liquor in any legislature." Pennsylvania, whose effort was spearheaded by Doug Moorhead of North East, Pennsylvania, was the first state to pass a "Limited Winery" law in 1968.

Limited wineries became known as "farm wineries," and for the first time in the United States, a vineyardist did not have to go through the formal, expensive process of becoming a bonded winery to produce and sell wine. Leon Adams became known as the "father of farm wineries."

Early History of Winemaking in the Region

"In 1870, the Masson brothers [Joseph and Jules] served a new sparkling blend of Delaware and Catawba to a meeting of the Pleasant Valley Grape Growers Association. Presiding at the meeting was famed horticulturist Colonel Marshall Winder of Boston, who on tasting the wine exclaimed: 'Truly, this will be the great champagne of the West!' By 'West,' Wilder explained he meant 'our entire continent,' the New World. His remark gave Great Western champagne its name, strange though it seems for a product of New York State.

In 1873 at the Vienna Exposition, Great Western became the first American champagne to win a gold medal in Europe, and it later gathered additional prizes at Brussels, Philadelphia, and [at the Exposition Universale in] Paris."

Leon Adams in *The Wines of America*

In 1829 in the rectory garden of St. James Episcopal Church in Hammondsport, Reverend William Bostwick introduced the first grapevines to the Finger Lakes Region. He planted Catawba and Isabella vines from the Hudson River Valley. In 1853, Andrew Reisinger, a German vineyardist, planted two acres of Catawba and Isabella vines in Pulteney, north of Hammondsport, for which he used trellises; he became a pioneer in training grapevines.

In his 1908 book, *The Grapes of New York,* U. P. Hedrick observed of Reisinger: "Reisinger trained, pruned, and tilled his vines, operations unheard of before in the district, and was rewarded with crops and profits which stimulated grape culture in his and nearby neighborhoods."

The first bonded Finger Lakes Region winery was Pleasant Valley Winery, producer of Great Western Champagne, which began commercial production of wine in 1860 in Pleasant Valley, south of Hammondsport. Charles Champlin, the French winemaker who founded Pleasant Valley Winery, was granted U.S. Winery License No. 1. The Urbana Wine Company, renamed Gold Seal Winery in 1887, was founded in 1865 by Guy McMaster and Clark Bell. In 1880, Walter Taylor and his wife, Adie, founded Taylor Wine Company and began to produce wine.

In 1848, Edward McKay planted 150 Isabella grapevines at Naples, at the southern end of Canandaigua Lake. The vines prospered, and an industry grew.

John Jacob Widmer, founder of Widmer Wine Cellars, and his wife, Lisette, emigrated from the Swiss village of Sherz in 1882. They planted vineyards immediately upon their arrival in Naples and began making wine as soon as their vineyards matured. They applied for a loan to expand their winery from the local banker, Hiram Maxfield. Maxfield, who owned a local winery, denied their request for a loan; he did not want to encourage competition. The Widmers obtained a loan from a nearby bank.

In 1910, the Widmers' son, Will, attended the Royal Wine

School at Geisenheim, Germany. Widmer was one of the first wineries in the United States to offer "varietal" wines of one grape variety, as opposed to generic wines, and also was among the first to offer dated vintage wines. In 1933, Will Widmer, president of Widmer Wine Cellars, bought out the rival Maxfield Cellars, whose founder had turned down his parents' request for a loan 50 years previously.

During Prohibition, 27 wineries went out of business. Taylor and Widmer survived by making and selling grape juice and sacramental wine. The three sons of Walter and Adie Taylor, Greyton, Clarence, and Fred, purchased the Columbia Wine Company in Pleasant Valley and moved the Taylor operation to its stately, stone headquarters building.

In 1934, president E. S. Underhill, Jr., of Gold Seal Vineyards, brought Charles Fournier, chief winemaker of Clicquot Ponsardin in Rheims, France, to Hammondsport as production manager to restore the winery's pre-Prohibition reputation. Fournier, educated at the University of Paris and at schools of enology in France and Switzerland, brought French-American hybrid grapes, initially Ravat 6 (Ravat Blanc) and Seibel 1000 (Rosette), to area vineyards.

In 1943, Fournier successfully introduced his champagne, Charles Fournier Brut, to the U.S. market. In 1950, the California State Fair opened its wine competition to eastern and foreign wines. The only gold medal awarded was for Charles Fournier New York State Champagne. In subsequent years, no non-California wines were allowed to compete at the State Fair in Sacramento.

In 1953, Fournier hired Dr. Konstantin Frank to establish a *Vitis vinifera* grape nursery at Gold Seal. Dr. Frank, who had been doing menial jobs, such as hoeing blueberries, at the New York State Agricultural Experiment Station at Geneva, was also hired as a consultant to Gold Seal.

Dr. Frank had seen *Vitis vinifera* grape varieties grown in the Ukraine where winters were as cold or colder than the Finger Lakes Region. He convinced Fournier that past problems growing European varieties of grapes in the Finger Lakes Region were due to diseases, such as mildew, which could be controlled. Winter temperatures were not the principal problem. In addition, Dr. Frank suggested grafting *Vitis vinifera* vines onto hardy rootstock that would allow the canes of the vine to ripen before the first winter freeze.

Gold Seal vineyardists began to graft *Vitis vinifera* vines onto hardy rootstock obtained from the garden of a convent in Quebec. The first real test came in February 1957 when the temperature plunged to 25 degrees below zero. Many *Vitis labrusca* varieties, particularly Dutchess and Isabella, had 100% bud damage. However, the grafted *Vitis vinifera* vines experienced only 10% bud damage. Fournier and Frank knew that their experiment had been successful.

In 1976, the New York State Legislature passed the Farm Winery Act. Removing the requirement for bonded wineries stimulated the Finger Lakes wine industry. Many vineyardists began to make wine instead of selling all of their grapes to wineries. By the early 21st century, over 70 wineries flourished in the Finger Lakes Region.

INTRODUCTION

Description of Grape Varieties

"More and more producers have become familiar with which grape variety grows where and are increasingly trying out new combinations of grapes, grape varieties new to a particular area, or deliberately searching out old vines, capable of producing top quality juice, of grape types that may be obscure or archaic, but may be well worth cherishing. They can also choose from the scores of new grape varieties that have been deliberately developed by grape breeders during the last 100 years, designed for special purposes and conditions."

Jancis Robinson in *Guide to Wine Grapes*

Species of Grapes

Vitis aestivalis—wild grape varieties occasionally used for making wine. The best-known *Vitis aestivalis* varieties are Cynthiana, Herbemont, Lenoir, and Norton. It is grown in most states bordering upon or east of the Mississippi River.

Vitis labrusca—hardy grape varieties known for their foxy or grapey taste. *Vitis labrusca* varieties include Catawba, Concord, Delaware, Elvira, and Niagara. The specie is grown in most states east of the Mississippi River.

Vitis riparia—herbaceous grape varieties that can be used to make high-acid wine. *Vitis riparia*, which has sturdy root-stock suitable for grafting, grows in the wild in Canada and in the Eastern United States, north of the Gulf states and the South Atlantic states. Baco Noir is probably the best-known *Vitis riparia* hybrid.

Vitis rotundifolia—popular grape varieties for wine and grape jelly in the South. *Vitis rotundifolia*, which is also known as Muscadine, varieties include Carlos, Magnolia, Noble, and Scuppernong. This specie is grown in all Gulf states and South Atlantic states.

Vitis rupestris—grows in Appalachia and in hilly soil west of the Mississippi River. This specie grows on rocky and hilly locations but does not like moist sites. The vines are vigorous and bushy, have deep roots, and are tolerant of alkaline soil.

Vitis vinifera—the classic "European" varieties of grapes considered to be the best in the world for winemaking, such as Cabernet Sauvignon, Chardonnay, Gewürztraminer, Pinot Noir, and Riesling. *Vitis vinifera* is widely grown in Europe and the United states, including the states of California, New York, Oregon, and Washington.

Vitis Vinifera Varieties for Red Wine

Alicante Bouschet—also known as Alicante and is occasionally used as a synonym for Grenache. Alicante Bouschet has intense color and is popular as a teinturier. It is an early ripening variety used mainly for blending.

Barbera—makes a heavy bodied wine with a distinct aroma that develops character with age. Barbera, a productive variety with a high level of natural acidity but good balance, is widely grown in Italy, particularly in the Piedmont.

Cabernet Franc—a French variety frequently blended with the later maturing Cabernet Sauvignon. Cabernet Franc is aromatic and tends to be lighter in color, body, and tannin than Cabernet Sauvignon, and it ripens in a cooler environment. Cabernet Franc usually makes a light-bodied or medium-bodied wine. Its vines are vigorous and fairly productive.

Cabernet Sauvignon—the world's most prestigious grape variety for the production of fine wine that ages well. It is the principal grape variety in Bordeaux wine in which it is blended with other varieties such as Merlot, Malbec, and Cabernet Franc to make a mellower wine. Cabernet Sauvignon, which is known for its deep color, high tannin, and flavor of black currants or eucalyptus, ages well in French oak. Its vines are vigorous but not particularly productive. It is a late ripening variety.

Carignane—an extremely productive grape variety that originated in Spain but is not widely grown there today. Because it ripens late, Carignane is suited only to relatively hot climates. Wine made from Carignane grapes has deep color, good body, and a clean flavor; it usually is high in acidity and tannin. Its vines are vigorous but not very disease resistant.

Carmine—in 1976, Dr. H. P. Olmo, plant geneticist emeritus of the University of California at Davis, developed this Cabernet Sauvignon-Carignane-Merlot cross attempting to combine the distinctive Cabernet taste and the productivity of Carignane with the mellowness of Merlot. Vines from an early planting in Georgia produced grapes from which a quality wine reminiscent of a Cabernet-Merlot blend was made.

Gamay—the grape of the Beaujolais region of France is one of numerous Gamay clones, many of which have been used as teinturiers. Gamay vines have a tendency to overbear; the grapes ripen early. The juice, which is relatively high in acidity, is usually vinified quickly and marketed as Beaujolais Nouveau. Beaujolais wine is meant to be drunk young; storing in a wine cellar for more than two or three years is not recommended. Two variations are grown in California: Napa Gamay and Gamay Beaujolais, a Pinot Noir clone.

Grenache—originated in Spain and is widely planted in Spain and southern France. The variety ripens early and is able to withstand heat and drought. Grenache, which is frequently blended with varieties higher in color and tannin, is popular with rosé producers, including those in the Tavel district of France. Its vines are vigorous and productive.

Lambrusco—a robust vine grown principally in the three central provinces of Italy. Wine made from this variety, which is extremely productive, is fruity, frothy, and meant to be drunk young. Lambrusco wine made in the United States is usually slightly sweet.

Lemberger—a German grape also known as Limberger and Blauer Limberger that is called Blauerfränkisch in Austria. Lemberger, which has notable color and acidity, is usually blended with Trollinger to produce a light-bodied red wine intended to be consumed young. The State of Washington has sizable plantings of Lemberger.

Malbec—a variety rich in tannin and color that is blended with Cabernet Sauvignon in Bordeaux wine. It is declining in popularity in France because it has many of the disadvantages of Merlot, such as not being very disease resistant. Also, Malbec doesn't have Merlot's high level of fruit quality. Most Malbec grown in California is blended into Meritage wines to simulate Bordeaux wine. Its vines are moderately productive.

Merlot—known for years as a blending variety, along with Cabernet Franc and, decreasingly, Malbec, in Bordeaux wine to complement the late-maturing and less mellow Cabernet Sauvignon. Merlot has become a popular variety on its own merit. It is widely planted in the cool, damp soils of St. Émilion and Pomerol; Cabernet Sauvignon prefers the well-drained soils of Médoc. Merlot is fruitier, less tannic, and more full-bodied than its sophisticated and long-lived blending partner. The wine usually has a strawberry or raspberry aroma. It is a vigorous, productive variety that ripens in mid-season.

Meunier—also known as Pinot Meunier, it is thought to be an early mutation of Pinot Noir. It was called Meunier (French for miller) because the underside of its leaves look like they have been dusted with flour. In Germany, it is known as Müllerrebe and Schwarzriesling. The variety is productive and winter hardy. Meunier, along with Chardonnay and Pinot Noir, is a component of the classic champagne blend. Pinot Blanc occasionally is the fourth variety in the cuvée. Chardonnay provides complexity to the blend, Pinot Noir the heaviness, and Meunier the fruity flavor.

Nebbiolo—grown principally in the Piedmont region of Italy, the variety is a late ripener that is very dependent upon the soil in which it is grown. When growing conditions are favorable, Nebbiolo wine is among the world's finest and long-lived; it tends to be high in color, tannin, and acidity while young, maturing into a wine with a notable bouquet. Wines made in Barbaresco and Barolo are the best-known Nebbiolo wines. The quality of these wines has motivated winemakers around the world to experiment with the variety.

Petite Sirah—a variety principally grown in California and Argentina that is probably not related to the true Syrah or a sub-variety of Syrah called Petite Syrah in France. Petite Sirah is occasionally blended with lighter red wines such as Zinfandel in California, where it has been grown since the 1880s. The wine is deep colored and robust with a touch of spicy, sometimes peppery, flavor. It is astringent with a pronounced aroma. High tannin makes the variety potentially suitable for aging.

Pinot Noir—the classic grape of Burgundy. Unlike Bordeaux wine, which is a blend, Burgundy is made from Pinot Noir grapes. Pinot Noir is difficult to grow, has low yield, and is very dependent on the type of soil in which it is grown. In *Guide to Wine Grapes,* Jancis Robinson observes: "If Cabernet wines appeal to the head, Pinot's charms are decidedly more sensual and more transparent." Pinot Noir is more fruity and has less tannin and pigment than Cabernet Sauvignon. When young, Pinot Noir has a taste of strawberries or cherries. Aged Pinot Noir usually has a velvety finish. It ripens early and is best grown in cool climates. Pinot Noir is widely grown in California; Oregon also has favorable growing conditions for the variety.

Ruby Cabernet—a cross of Carignane and Cabernet Sauvignon that reached the peak of its popularity in California in the 1960s. In 1949, Dr. H. P. Olmo of the University of California at Davis attempted to combine the high yield and heat tolerance of Carignane with the quality of

Cabernet Sauvignon with this hybrid. Although it was meant to be a claret-type wine made from grapes grown in hot growing regions, it has done well in cooler growing climates. South Central San Joaquin Valley is one of the regions of California in which it is grown. It is a heavy bearer in South Africa and is grown in limited quantities in Australia.

Sangiovese—is heavily planted in central Italy and is the principal grape for red wine in Tuscany. The variety tends to be high in tannin and acid but not color; it varies widely, depending upon vineyard location. Brunello di Montalcino wine is made from Sangiovese; it is one of the grape varieties used in making Chianti. Literally translated, Sangiovese is "blood of Jove." The variety grows well in a range of soils, but it is particularly suited to limestone soil. It blends well with Cabernet Sauvignon. Sangiovese ripens late; it tends to be relatively high in alcohol and to be long-lived in hot growing seasons. In cool growing seasons, high tannin is a problem along with high acidity.

Zinfandel—grown primarily in California, the variety has been cultivated there since the 1850s. Zinfandel was grown in North Coast vineyards and was popular with gold miners in California in the mid-1800s. It is known as Primivito di Gioia at Apulia in the heel of Italy. Although it is grown in hot climates, Zinfandel improves when grown in a cool climate that ensures a long growing season, and when productivity is limited. The variety ripens unevenly, with green berries and ripe berries in the same bunch. Zinfandel is not considered a noble grape; however, it makes a red wine with rich body, good flavor, and a sweet bouquet. The wine has a life of four to eight years. Occasionally, it is blended with Petite Sirah. In the late 1980s, surplus Zinfandel grapes were used to make White Zinfandel, which became a marketing success. The crisp, fruity wine is made by leaving the fermenting juice in contact with the skins for only a short period of time.

Vitis Vinifera Varieties for White Wine

Aligoté—a productive grape principally grown in Burgundy where Chardonnay predominates. Aligoté makes a tart wine not suitable for oak-aging that is characteristically high in acid, low in tannin, and is best consumed young. The variety's vines are vigorous, but yields vary widely. Aligoté is widely grown in Bulgaria and Rumania, as well as Russia, Ukraine, Georgia, and Moldova.

Chardonnay—the variety of White Burgundy. With the increased use of varietal names in the late twentieth century, Chardonnay has become a universally known grape variety. It produces high yields in a wide variety of vineyard locations; in fact, its productivity must be limited to ensure quality. Chardonnay is a fairly vigorous variety that matures early. It is suitable for climates with a short to medium growing season; it is moderately winter hardy. The variety is popular for its wide range of tastes, usually the fruity flavor of apples, melons, or pears. A wide range of winemaking techniques is used to produce Chardonnay. It can be bottled early after a long, cool fermentation process as with Moselle and Vouvray or aged in oak. It may have a nutty or buttery flavor. The variety is widely used in making champagne; its varietal taste is not lost when blended. It ages well in the bottle for two or more decades, but it is not as long-lived as Riesling.

Chenin Blanc—widely grown in the cool Loire region of France. It is considered a quality wine in Anjou-Touraine, where its yield is limited, and the climate and soil are ideal. In California, it is predominately grown in the hot Central Valley where it loses some of its honey flavor. It is a versatile, productive grape with considerable bouquet and relatively high acidity. Chenin Blanc makes a fresh, light, fruity wine with a wide range of sweetness; it is frequently blended, usually with Colombard, sometimes with Sémillon. The variety is also used in producing sparkling wine.

Colombard—also known as French Colombard. Its popularity has waned in recent years, and Colombard vines are being pulled from vineyards in France and in California's Central Valley. The variety was frequently used as a clean, pleasant but neutral component of blends. Originally, Colombard was used in France, along with Ugni Blanc and Folle Blanche, in making Cognac. In California, it was also used to make brandy. Most of the Colombard in France is north and west of the Bordeaux region in Bourg and Blaye. It ripens in midseason.

Gewürztraminer—a light-bodied to medium-bodied white wine known for its notable aroma. The German word "gewürz," meaning spiced, is the usual way of describing the wine. It tends to be crisp with a bouquet of tropical fruit. Gewürztraminer wine has higher than average alcohol content and can be cellared for medium-term aging. It is a difficult variety to grow and with its small bunches is not considered a high-yield grape. It is a particularly suitable grape for the soil and growing season of Alsace, and it is very popular there. The variety grows well in rich, clay soils, such as those in the Haut-Rhin départmente. It ripens in early midseason. Washington and Oregon also provide a favorable growing climate for Gewürztraminer.

Muscat Ottonel—the palest of the Muscat varieties has a less grapey aroma than other Muscat grapes. This low-yield grape ripens early and grows well in deep, damp soils in a cool climate. Little Muscat other than Muscat Ottonel is grown in Alsace, where it is made into a dry wine. Muscat Ottonel is grown in Austria, Hungary, Rumania, Russia, and the Ukraine. Small quantities of the variety are grown in the Finger Lakes Region. Occasionally it is used to make sparkling wine.

Pinot Blanc—widely planted in France, it is a mutation of Pinot Gris, which is a relative of Pinot Noir. The variety is not particularly productive, but new clones have higher yields than early Pinot Blancs. It is widely cultivated in Alsace and in Germany. Pinot Blanc is relatively full-bodied but is not known for its aroma or for being long-lived.

Pinot Gris—called Pinot Grigio in Italy, it is a widely planted grape that makes soft wine with body and color and a mildly perfumed bouquet. Pinot Gris is one of the best-known mutations of Pinot Noir. Its leaves are identical to Pinot Noir leaves, and the appearance of the berries is similar to Pinot Noir berries late in the growing season. Pinot Gris wine is made with a wide range of sweetness. It is a popular wine in Alsace, where it is a dry wine that is not overpowered by hearty food. It is called Tokay in Alsace. In some growing regions, it is low in acidity.

Riesling—one of the world's premier wine grapes because of its longevity and its ability to retain its style wherever it is grown. Riesling wine, which has a desirable level of acidity, is made with a wide range of sweetness. Riesling made with higher levels of sweetness has probably lessened the variety's reputation compared with other varieties, such as Chardonnay. The taste of Riesling is sometimes described as steely with an aroma of flowers, honey, or tropical fruit. The wine is light-bodied or medium-bodied. Riesling vines are winter hardy, making it a suitable *Vitis vinifera* variety for growing in cool regions. It is moderately vigorous and ripens in late midseason. Riesling is also used in making ice wine pressed from frozen grapes. The variety is grown in Alsace where Riesling is a prime example of its specialty, dry wine from aromatic grapes. It is widely planted in Australia, where the climate is suitable for growing Riesling grapes.

Rkatsiteli—a little-known grape considered to be a Russian variety but whose origins were probably on the border between Armenia and Turkey near Mt. Ararat. It is widely grown in the countries of the former Soviet Union, particularly Georgia, Ukraine, and Moldova. It is also grown in Bulgaria and Rumania. Rkatsiteli is known for having a touch of spiciness, similar to but different from Gewürztraminer. It is relatively high in acid with high sugar levels; its vines are winter hardy, making it a desirable variety for cool or cold regions. Small quantities of the variety are grown in the Finger Lakes Region.

Sauvignon Blanc—the white-wine grape of Bordeaux that is the source for well-known dry white wines such as Pouilly-Fumé and Sancerre from France and Fumé-Blanc produced in California. It makes a crisp and aromatic wine with a herbaceous taste. It is frequently blended with Sémillon. This zesty wine is intended to be drunk young except when aged in oak, which requires an additional year or two of cellaring. The variety, which is known for vigorous vine growth, is widely grown in the regions of Entre-Deux-Mers, Graves, and Sauternes in France. The vine is particularly suitable to the limestone vineyards of the Loire. Robert Mondavi named California wine made with Sauvignon Blanc grapes "Fumé-Blanc." It ripens in midseason. The variety is popular in South Africa and is also grown in the State of Washington.

Sémillon—its reputation is based upon the dry and sweet wines of Bordeaux, particularly in Sauternes and Graves, where it is frequently blended with Sauvignon Blanc and occasionally with Muscadelle. Sémillon, known for its body and lack of aroma, complements Sauvignon Blanc, which tends to have light body, high acid levels, and a strong aroma. Sémillon has been blended with Chardonnay in response to a demand for Chardonnay that exceeded the supply. Sémillon vines are vigorous, producing high grape yields. It is less winter hardy than Riesling and Chardonnay. The variety is widely grown in South America and Australia.

Ugni Blanc—known as Trebbiano in Italy and St. Émilion in the Cognac region of France, is vigorous and is the most widely planted grape variety in France. It is known for high yields, high levels of acidity, and relatively low alcohol content. Wine made from Ugni Blanc grapes is light and crisp but unfortunately neutral. Ugni Blanc is the staple of the French and Spanish brandy industries and is the principal ingredient of Armagnac. Ugni Blanc is widely planted in Italy and South America.

Viognier—the grape variety whose reputation is based on the highly regarded wine, Condrieu, that is high in color, acid, and aroma. Its flavor is reminiscent of apricots and peaches. However, the wine is low in acid and is usually drunk young. Viognier vines can be cultivated in dry growing conditions. The variety is increasingly being planted in California and in Australia.

French-American Hybrid Varieties for Red Wine

Baco Noir—a hybrid of Folle Blanche and a *Vitis riparia* variety, it is medium-bodied to full-bodied and is relatively high in acidity. Baco Noir has deep color and benefits from aging. When young, it has strong character reminiscent of Cabernet Sauvignon; however, it is frequently described as having a smokey taste and a fruity, black pepper aroma. The variety, which ripens early, is vigorous, disease resistant, and moderately winter hardy. It is widely grown in the United States in the East and Midwest and in Canada.

Chambourcin—of uncertain parentage, it is popular in the Loire Valley and the Touraine Region of France, probably because it has some of the characteristics of Cabernet Franc. It can be made into quality red wine as well as pleasant rosé wine. Chambourcin vines are vigorous and disease resistant. The variety ripens in late midseason and therefore is suited to regions with long growing seasons. It is rich in color and body but has little aroma.

Chancellor—initially called Seibel 7053 for the hybridizer, it was widely grown in France. In recent years, many French-American hybrid vines, including Chancellor, have been pulled out and replaced in French vineyards. It is a productive variety that makes well-balanced wine with deep color and is suitable for blending and for wood-aging. It is susceptible to downy mildew. Chancellor grows well in cool climates and is well represented in vineyards in the Finger Lakes Region.

Chelois—another Seibel hybrid, it makes a Burgundy-style hearty red wine with good balance that ages well and is a desirable ingredient of a full-bodied blend. It is lightly fla-vored and has a mild bouquet. In deep, well-drained soil, its vines are vigorous and provide a high yield. It is disease resis-tant and moderately winter hardy. Substantial plantings of

31

Chelois have been made in the Eastern United States, particularly when early midseason ripening is required.

Colobel—a teinturier, it is not usually made as a varietal wine. It has three to five times (up to 10 times) the color intensity of average red wine. It blends well; however, in France, where authorized, the legal limit of Colobel addition is five percent. The variety is fairly vigorous and productive. It ripens in midseason. The vines are moderately winter hardy.

DeChaunac—a Seibel hybrid, the variety is vigorous, productive, disease resistant, and winter hardy. It ripens early. In the early 1970s, thousands of acres of DeChaunac were planted to fill the demand for a basic red-wine grape. However, overplanting occurred; the real demand was for white grapes. Many DeChaunac vines producing low quality fruit were pulled out and replaced with other varieties. Canadian viticulturalist Adhemar DeChaunac, for whom the variety is named, preferred Chelois.

Landot—Landot 4511, a cross of Landot 244 (Landal) x Villard Blanc, is designed to combine the excellent red-wine qualities of Landal with the vigor and high yield of Villard Blanc. Landot is vigorous, productive, and disease resistant. It has an agreeable aroma; however, its wine quality is slightly inferior to Landal, which gives only moderate yields but produces a Beaujolais-type wine with deep color.

Léon Millot—a cousin of Maréchal Foch, it is more vigorous, more productive, and the wine has a deeper color than its relative. It ripens early and is a good choice for growing in regions with short growing seasons. The variety is disease resistant and winter hardy. It produces a good varietal wine, and it is suitable for blending.

Maréchal Foch—named for the World War I French general, it was originally called Kuhlmann 188-2. The variety is an Alsatian cross of Pinot Noir x Gamay x *Vitis riparia* that produces a Burgundy-type wine without the complexity. Maréchal Foch has a strong, somewhat herbaceous flavor and a deep color. It develops a fruity bouquet reminiscent of claret. The vines are vigorous, disease resistant, and winter hardy. The variety ripens early, is suitable for cool climates, and therefore grows well where the growing season is short. The strong Maréchal Foch character can be moderated by nouveau-style carbonic maceration.

Rosette—known initially as Seibel 1000, it was one of the first French-American hybrids grown in New York State. Its vines are winter hardy and vigorous, but yield is moderate. Rosette makes a neutral wine of good quality; however, it lacks the deep color of some of the other hybrids and is usually used to make rosé wine. Its popularity has declined, and it is being replaced by other varieties.

Rougeon—used primarily as a teinturier and in blends because of its high color; however, it is not as intense a teinturier as Colobel. It is grown in the Finger Lakes Region where occasionally it is made as a varietal wine. Rougeon is an early midseason grape with erratic production—a large quantity of fruit one year, very little the next. Its vines are vigorous.

Note: Maurice Baco, Georges Couderc, M. Louis Seibel, and Seyve-Villard were among the early hybridizers in France. Later hybridizers included Kuhlmann, Landot, Johannes-Seyve, and Vidal.

French-American Hybrid Varieties for White Wine

Aurora—ripens early and is usually picked the first week of September in the Finger Lakes Region. The variety does well in cool climates and is suitable for regions with short growing seasons. The vines are vigorous and winter hardy. The wine has a delicate, fruity flavor with a recognizable aroma and some residual sugar. It has moderate alcohol, is well balanced, and is frequently used for blending.

Cayuga White—a New York State Agricultural Experiment Station cross of Seyval Blanc x Schuyler, which is a hybrid of Zinfandel and Ontario. Ontario is a cross of Winchell x Diamond. The vine is vigorous, moderately hardy, and disease resistant. The wine has a pleasant, apple-like fruity flavor and is well-balanced with a delicate aroma. It is medium-bodied with a pleasant aftertaste. It resembles Riesling.

Chardonel—a New York State Agricultural Experiment Station cross of Seyval Blanc x Chardonnay. Chardonel, which requires a longer than average growing season, is moderately winter hardy—more hardy than its Chardonnay parent. The variety ripens late, has a high yield, and retains good acid balance during ripening that makes it suitable for sparkling wine production. The wine is clean and crisp with a Chardonnay character. It is usually described as pleasant with a delicate, fruity flavor.

Horizon—a New York State Agricultural Experiment Station sister seedling of Cayuga White, a cross of Seyval Blanc x Schuyler. The variety, which is suitable for cool growing climates, outperforms Aurora and Cayuga White in the vineyard. The grapes have low acidity and a neutral flavor; the wine, which is suitable for blending, is usually rated above Aurora but below Cayuga White in quality.

Melody—a New York State Agricultural Experiment Station cross of Seyval Blanc x Geneva White 5, which is a cross of Pinot Blanc x Ontario. The vines are vigorous, productive, and moderately winter hardy, similar to Seyval Blanc. Melody grapes ripen in late midseason and produce wine with varietal character that has a neutral, fruity flavor with a hint of herbs and a flowery aroma.

Rayon d'Or—a Seibel hybrid with a spicy, fruity taste that makes a pleasant still wine or sparkling wine. It is also used in blends. The variety ripens in early midseason and is capable of high sugar content in cool growing regions. Rayon d'Or wine has a notable aroma and a raspberry taste. The variety is disease resistant and moderately winter hardy. It is widely grown in France.

Seyval Blanc—has fairly vigorous, productive vines that are moderately winter hardy. Initially, the wine was dry, flinty, and made in the Chablis style. A wider range of styles is used today, including wine with a touch of sweetness. The wine is delicate with a notable bouquet and an excellent sugar-acid balance. It has an apple, citrus, or melon flavor. The wine is light-bodied to medium-bodied with a crisp finish.

Verdelet—has healthy vines of average vigor. The grapes are delicate and ripen in early midseason. The wine has a light aroma similar to Gewürztraminer, is well-balanced, and has good flavor. The variety has a pronounced, delicate bouquet and low acidity. It is sometimes aged in oak, after which it develops its own character imparted by the type of soil and climate. Verdelet is not widely planted in the Finger Lakes Region.

Vidal Blanc—a hybrid of the grape called St. Émilion in the Cognac district of France, Ugni Blanc in southern France, and Trebbiano in Tuscany in Italy with Rayon d'Or, which is grown widely in the Loire Valley of France. The vines are vigorous, productive, disease resistant, and winter hardy. It is a late-ripening variety that grows well in cool climates. The wine has the pleasant character of the St. Émilion grape and a touch of spiciness and high alcohol content similar to Rayon d'Or. When fermented with German yeast, it resembles Riesling. It is high in acid, causing some residual sugar to be necessary to produce a balanced wine. It is suitable for producing late harvest wine and ice wine. The wine has a delicate flavor and bouquet with a fine aroma.

Vignoles—a cross of Seibel 6905 hybrid x Pinot Noir. It is also called Ravat 51. The vines are vigorous and moderately hardy but yield is low because the bunches are small. The grapes ripen in early midseason. The variety produces a clean, crisp, well-balanced wine capable of a subtle fineness with a distinct bouquet. Vignoles makes wine of high quality similar to Chablis; it is suitable for making champagne.

Villard Blanc—a late-ripening Seyve-Villard cross. The vine is vigorous, productive, and winter hardy but suitable for warm climates and long growing seasons. It was widely planted in southern France in the 1950s and 1960s because of its high yield. Villard Blanc produces a neutral, soft wine with good body that is meant to be consumed young. It is considered a good variety for blending.

Traminette—a University of Illinois cross of Seyve 23.416 hybrid x Gewürztraminer. This productive variety ripens in late midseason and is moderately winter hardy—more hardy than its Gewürztraminer parent. Traminette has an average-length growing season. It produces wine of good body, superior quality, and excellent sugar-acid balance with the distinct bouquet and spicy character of Gewürztraminer. Wines are finished dry or semi-dry depending on preference.

Native-American Grapes (Vitis Labrusca)

Catawba—was the foremost wine grape in the United States in the 1800s. The vine is vigorous and productive but not particularly hardy or disease resistant. This white variety ripens in midseason and is frequently used as a blend in champagne. Catawba wine is made in a wide diversity of styles. The variety has a high sugar content and high acidity. It has a clean taste and a spicy aroma. Its slightly tart flavor occurs occasionally as an aftertaste.

Concord—the most widely grown variety in New York State. This red-grape variety is principally grown for juice and jelly. Its dominant foxy, grapey taste makes it unsuitable for wine, and its powerful aroma makes it undesirable for blending. The vine is hardy, vigorous, productive, and disease resistant. Concord ripens in midseason. It is occasionally used in making port and sherry.

Cynthiana—makes wine with intense color and a distinctive, pleasant aroma. It usually acquires bouquet with aging.

Delaware—is a highly regarded native white-wine grape with high sugar and only a moderate *Vitis labrusca* flavor. The vine is winter hardy but not particularly vigorous. Delaware grows in a wide range of soils. The variety produces a light, flowery-fruity, dry or semi-sweet wine with a delicious aroma. It is frequently used in champagne blends. Delaware is widely planted in Japan, probably because its early ripening quality is suited to Japan's damp autumns.

Diamond—a white variety also known as Moore's Diamond. In 1873, Jacob Moore of Brighton, New York, crossed Concord with Iona to create Diamond. It makes a fruity, piquant, high-quality wine.

Dutchess—the vines are not vigorous and are only moderately productive. It is grown in well-drained, moderately fertile soils. This white-grape variety ripens in early midseason. Duchess is known for low acid at low sugar levels and therefore makes a low-alcohol wine. It is suitable to oak-aging and is one of the few whites to improve with age, for at least 10 years. It makes a quality wine with a pleasant, delicate flavor with little *Vitis labrusca* in its aroma or character.

Elvira—the vine is healthy, vigorous, winter hardy, and moderately productive. This white-grape variety ripens early. The juice tends to be low in sugar and high in acid, giving the resulting wine a sharp aroma and a hard flavor. It is frequently used for blending.

Ives—is hardy, vigorous, productive, and disease resistant. The variety has deep-red color and ripens in midseason. The wine has a a strong foxy flavor that makes it too highly flavored and heavy for producing a varietal wine. It is used mainly for blending.

Isabella—the vine is healthy and vigorous with above average yield. It ripens in early midseason. It is rarely made into a varietal wine; it is usually blended. Occasionally, it is fermented on the skins to produce pink wine. The wine has a foxy, grapey flavor with a musky aroma. When pressed and fermented in white-wine style, the foxiness is reduced, and the resulting wine is pale, growing paler with age.

Niagara—the vine is very vigorous with extremely high production when grown in deep, rich soil. This white-grape variety ripens in early midseason. The wine is noticeably foxy and is usually made semi-sweet. Niagara wine is usually served very cold.

Norton—considered to be one of the better native-American wine grapes. It is sometimes blended with Ives.

Steuben—was developed at the New York State Agricultural Experiment Station and released in 1947. The blue-black grape produces a popular rosé. The wine is light, almost pink in color, and pleasant on the palate. It has a *Vitis labrusca* taste with a spicy fruitiness similar to Muscat.

Vincent—was developed by the Horticultural Research Institute of Ontario, Canada. The vines are vigorous, productive, and moderately winter hardy. The dark-blue grape produces deep-red-colored wine of high quality.

Grapes, Long Bunch

CHAPTER 1

Wineries West and North of the Finger Lakes

"And Noah he often said to his wife
When he sat down to dine,
'I don't care where the water goes if
it doesn't get into the wine.'"

Gilbert K. Chesterton, *Wine and Water*

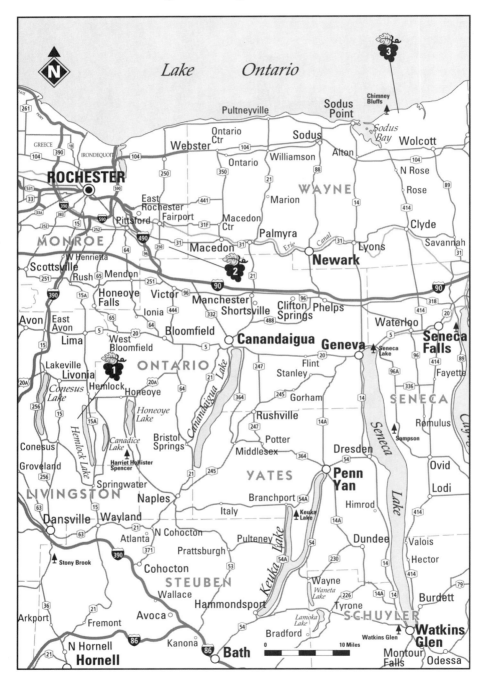

CHAPTER 1

Wineries West and North of the Finger Lakes

1. Eagle Crest Vineyards / O-Neh-Da Winery

Eagle Crest Vineyards and O-Neh-Da Winery are located at 7107 Vineyard Road, Conesus, NY 14435, (585) 346-2321. The Winery is one-half mile off Mission Road in Conesus-on-Hemlock. O-Neh-Da Winery was founded in 1872 by Bishop Bernard J. McQuaid, the first Catholic Bishop of Rochester, when he purchased a 527-acre farm above Hemlock Lake as a vacation retreat.

Bishop McQuaid began the Winery to supply his priests with wine for church services. By 1905, the Winery maintained 80 acres of vineyards and bottled 20,000 gallons of wine annually. The cellar, with two underground levels, was expanded to a capacity of 150,000 gallons.

Bishop McQuaid died in 1909, and the farm was bequeathed to St. Bernard's Seminary, which he had founded in 1893. His successor, Bishop Thomas F. Hickey, ran the farm and winery until 1924, when it became too burdensome.

Bishop Hickey sold the operation to the Society of the Divine Word, a missionary order. The Winery was closed during Prohibition. Only 20 acres of the vineyard were being cultivated when the Winery reopened in 1936. The Society, owners at the time of the nearby St. Michael's Seminary, refurbished the Winery and resumed making O-Neh-Da wines. Subsequently, the St. Michael's Seminary buildings were sold to the Church of the Restitution, a fundamentalist church.

By 1972, over 100 acres of grapes were under cultivation, and a sufficient amount of altar wine was being produced to supply the clergy throughout eastern United States. Stephen Goldstone owns and manages Eagle Crest Vineyards, Inc., which also bottles red, white, and pink blends with the Barry Winery label.

About 90 percent of the output of Eagle Crest Vineyards, Inc., is altar or sacramental wine. For over a century, these wines have been "ecclesiastically approved by the Bishop of Rochester." O-Neh-Da labels have included Angelica, Chalice White, Concord, Haute Sauterne, St. Michael's Red,

St. Michael's Rosé, Cream Sherry, and Pink Tokay.

The altar wines are sold directly to churches; they cannot be purchased or sampled by visitors to the Winery. White and rosé altar wines are more popular than red, because they do not stain the purificator used to clean the chalice during Mass.

The Winery is located in a rustic setting. The winetasting room is open year-round, Monday through Friday. Group tours and weekend tastings may be arranged by appointment.

2. Casa Larga Vineyards

Casa Larga Vineyards is located 15 miles south of Rochester at 2287 Turk Hill Road, Fairport, NY 14450, (585) 223-4210, www.casalarga.com. The winery has the appearance of a Tuscan villa, with Italian marble, stucco walls, sturdy arches, and vaulted ceilings. The winery is at the crest of Turk Hill, one of the highest points in Monroe County, and has a commanding view of the Rochester skyline.

The owners, Andrew and Ann Colaruotolo, planted their first vines in 1974 and by 1990 had 25 acres planted; Casa Larga has grown into a 40-acre estate winery. Andrew Colaruotolo, who is also the winemaker, is a successful Rochester area contractor. He grew up in Gaeta in the Frascati grapegrowing region of Italy and spent 20 years of his youth working in the family vineyard, also known as Casa Larga. He still works in the vineyard—the "new" Casa Larga vineyard. Their son, John, is the vineyard manager.

Casa Larga specializes in wine made from *Vitis vinifera*, or European-style grapes, such as full-bodied, oak-aged Cabernet Sauvignon and a Cabernet Sauvignon / Merlot blend; four Chardonnays: Reserve Chardonnay, aged in Rover oak; light Kaleidoscope Chardonnay, aged sur lies style; rich CLV Chardonnay; and crisp Vineyard Hill Chardonnay; as well as spicy, dry Alsatian-style Gewürztraminer; medium-bodied, oak-aged Pinot Noir; and a light, crisp Dry Riesling. The winery also grows French-American hybrid grapes, including Aurora, DeChaunac, and

45

Vidal Blanc, which is used to make a soft, dry, and lightly oaked dinner wine. DeChaunac is used in Petite Noir, a light, dry, and fruity Beaujolais-style wine.

In addition to their varietal wines, Casa Larga makes blends, including Lilac Hill, a smooth, fruity blend of Riesling and Muscat Ottonel; Blush, a blend of Aurora, DeChaunac, and Vidal Blanc; Estate Red, a hearty dinner wine aged in American oak; Estate White, a semi-dry blend of Vidal Blanc and *Vitis vinifera*; and Tapestry, a light, dry Cabernet Sauvignon / DeChaunac blend.

Casa Larga's specialty wines include Meritage, a blend of Merlot, Cabernet Sauvignon, and Cabernet Franc; Kaleidoscope Viognier wine with a fresh bouquet and a bright finish; and Fiori Delle Stelle Ice Wine, rich dessert wine made from Vidal Blanc grapes. Casa Larga also makes champagne, including rich, golden Blanc de Blancs Brut, a dry champagne made from Chardonnay in the *méthode champenoise*.

Casa Larga makes personalized wine labels for a nominal charge. "Bottled Especially for ... " and "Bottled to Celebrate the Anniversary (or Birthday) of ... " The winery is open seven days a week and has banquet / meeting facilities for groups by reservation. During the spring, summer, and fall, the winery provides picnic tables and complimentary grape juice for children.

3. Thorpe Vineyard

Thorpe Vineyard is located at 8150 Chimney Heights Blvd., Wolcott, NY 14590, (315) 594-2502. The vineyard was planted in 1978; the first harvest was in 1983. The winery's *Vitis vinifera* varietals include unoaked Chardonnay, a classic Pinot Noir, and Semi-dry Riesling. Thorpe Vineyard's wines produced from French-American hybrid grapes are medium-bodied Baco Noir with a touch of Pinot Noir for complexity, Maréchal Foch, a robust Chancellor, Cayuga White, and a crisp, dry Vidal Blanc.

Thorpe Vineyard's blends include Evening Glow, a dry blush wine with a subtle oak flavor made from Chardonnay and Pinot Noir; Fialka, a semi-sweet sipping wine with a soft bouquet and a smooth taste; and Lake Breeze, a blend of Vidal Blanc, Riesling, and Cayuga White. The winery also produces zesty Harvest Moon apple wine.

* * *

Lake Ontario Wine Trail
In 2001, the Lake Ontario Wine Trail was established. In addition to Thorpe Vineyard, the Wine Trail members are:

> North Country Apple Winery, (585) 594-2248
> 10555 Slaght Road
> Wolcott, NY 14490
(Apple juice, apple cider, apple wine blends)

> Giancarelli Brothers Winery, (315) 626-2830
> 10252 Shortcut Road
> Weedsport, NY 13166
(Blueberry, strawberry, elderberry dessert wines and blends)

> Martin's Honey Farm & Meadery, (315) 947-5965
> 14699 Center Road
> Sterling, NY 13156
(Mead [honey wine], fruit wine, and grape wine)

> Fruit Valley Orchard, (315) 342-3793
> 507 Bunker Hill Road
> Oswego, NY 13126
(Pear nectar, ice Fuji, and non-alcoholic gourmet juices)

> Ashley Lynn Winery, (315) 963-3262
> 4142 State Route 104
> Mexico, NY 13114
(Blended apple wines)

Canandaigua Lake Vineyards

CHAPTER 2

Canandaigua Lake Wineries

"Quickly, bring me a beaker of wine, so that I may wet my mind
and say something clever."

Aristophanes

"A man will be eloquent if you give him good wine."

Ralph Waldo Emerson, "Monthigne,"
Representative Men, 1850

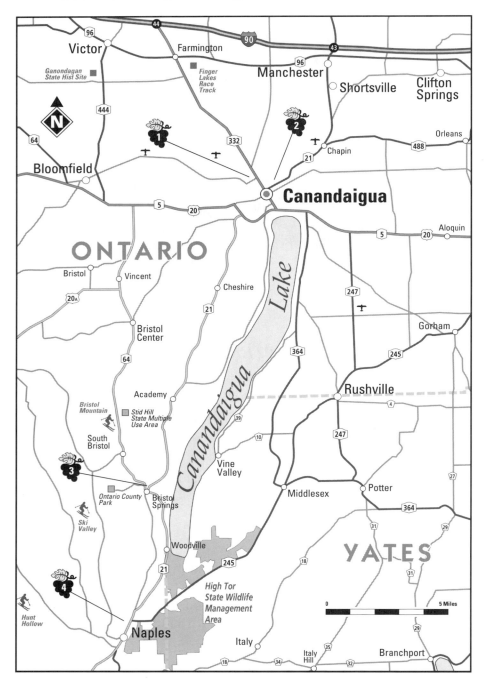

CHAPTER 2

Canandaigua Lake Wineries

1. Canandaigua Wine Company

Canandaigua Wine Company is located at 235 N. Bloomfield Road, Canandaigua, NY, (585) 394-7900, www.cwine.com. Constellation Brands, Inc., is the parent of Canandaigua Wine Company. In 2003, with the acquisition of Australia's BRL Hardy, Ltd., Canandaigua Wine Company became the largest wine company in the U.S.

Constellation Brands owns wineries in California, including Paul Masson, Mission Bell, Turner Road, Cribari, Dunnewood, Escalon, and Riverland Vineyards. Almaden, Inglenook, Talus, Vendange, Columbia, Cook's, Covey Run, Ravenswood, Ste. Chappelle, and Taylor Reserve are also Canandaigua Wine Company labels.

Unlike most wineries, Canandaigua Wine Company sells no wine with the Company's name on the label. Canandaigua Wine makes J. Roget charmat-process champagne and distributes Argentinian wines (Marcus James) as well as German wines (Keller-Geister).

In 1987, Canandaigua Wine Company purchased Widmer Wine Cellars of Naples, New York, and the Monarch Wine Company of Brooklyn, known for its Manischewitz kosher wines. Canandaigua closed the Monarch Winery in Brooklyn and moved the production of Manischewitz to Widmer to bring the Naples winery production closer to its capacity.

2. Finger Lakes Wine Center at Sonnenberg Gardens

The Finger Lakes Wine Center is located in Bay House at Sonnenberg Gardens, 151 Charlotte Street, Canandaigua, NY 14424, (585) 394-9016, www.fingerlakeswinecenter.com. In 2002, the Wine Center retailed over 178 wines for 30 Finger Lakes wineries. The Wine Center also markets its own wine with the Sonnenberg label, including Sonnenberg Mary Red, a blend of Rougeon, Maréchal Foch, Vignoles, and Vincent; and Sonnenberg Garden Rosé, a Baco Noir / Cayuga White blend. The Wine Center offers winetastings and stocks a wide variety of wine-related gifts and gourmet food.

3. Arbor Hill Grapery & Winery

Arbor Hill Grapery & Winery is located at 6461 Route 64, Naples, NY 14512, (585) 374-2870, www.thegrapery.com. The Winery, six miles north of Naples near the intersection of Routes 21 and 64, is owned by John and Katie Brahm. Arbor Hill Winery produces wine from European, French-American hybrid, and native-American grapes. The Brahms have over 17 acres of vineyards in production.

Arbor Hill's European or *Vitis vinifera* varietals are Chardonnay aged in French Nevers oak, Dry Riesling, and semi-dry Johannisberg Riesling; its hybrid wines include Cayuga White, Gewürztraminer-style Traminette, Vidal Blanc, Maréchal Foch, and Noir, a blend of Maréchal Foch and Chambourcin aged in French Nevers oak. Onnalinda White is a semi-dry blend of Cayuga White, Vidal Blanc, and Traminette that is similar to Chablis.

Arbor Hill also produces wine from native-American *Vitis labrusca* varieties, such as Catawba, Moore's Diamond, and Niagara. In addition, it makes sparkling wines, including Celebration, a blend of Cayuga White, Traminette, and Vidal Blanc.

Arbor Hill Grapery & Winery offers other grape products, including grape pies and grape pie filling, hot grape sundaes, wine jelly, wine preserves, wine sausage, and wine vinegar.

4. Widmer Wine Cellars

Widmer Wine Cellars, purchased by Canandaigua Wine Company in 1987, is located at 1 Lake Niagara Lane, Naples, NY 14512, (585) 374-6311, www.widmerwine.com. The winery has over 1,000 acres of vineyards in production.

Widmer is principally known for Lake Niagara white wine, Crackling Lake Niagara, ports, and sherries; however, it distributes other wines, including Cabernet Sauvignon, Pinot Noir, Chardonnay, Dry Riesling, Taylor Pink Catawba, Great Western Chardonnay Champagne, and the popular Arbor Mist fruit-flavored wines.

Widmer Wine Cellars has made Manischewitz kosher premium wines at its Naples facility since 1987. The Wine Cellars offers an informative winery tour, including a walking tour of the cool, underground cellars with large oak vats that is followed by an overview of the bottling facility. The Manischewitz bottling line is included on the tour, which is concluded with a winetasting in the Niagara Chalet. The Widmer Antique Museum displays a collection of old winemaking equipment along the tour route.

Widmer uses the "solera" process in making Sherry, similar to that used by the Sherry bodegas of Spain. A solera consists of tiers of Sherries of different ages. Sherry to be bottled is taken from the bottom tier, which contains the oldest wine. The barrels are left half-full and are filled from barrels from the second tier, which contain the second-oldest wine.

The process is repeated with the third tier, with the quantity withdrawn always replaced with the next oldest. The new Sherry always is put into the barrels on the top tier, thus continually blending new Sherry with aged Sherry. Sherry is rarely vintage dated because of this process of blending a number of years production.

The winery was one of the first in the United States to make "varietal" wines of one grape variety, as opposed to generic wines, and also was among the first to offer dated vintage wines. Visitors are invited to drive up Lake Niagara Lane for a breathtaking view of Widmer's vineyards and the Naples Valley. In the fall, foliage colors are spectacular.

* * *

Canandaigua Wine Trail

In 2001, the Canandaigua Wine Trail was established. Members of the Wine Trail are Widmer Wine Cellars, Arbor Hill Grapery & Winery, Finger Lakes Wine Center at Sonnenberg Gardens, and Casa Larga Vineyards in Fairport, north of Canandaigua Lake in southern Monroe County. The Trail's website is: www.canandaiguawinetrailonline.com.

CHAPTER 3

Keuka Lake Wineries — West Side

"So Life's year begins and closes;
　Days though shortening still can shine;
What though youth gave love and roses,
　Age still leaves us friends and wine."

Thomas More, *Spring and Autumn,* Stanza I

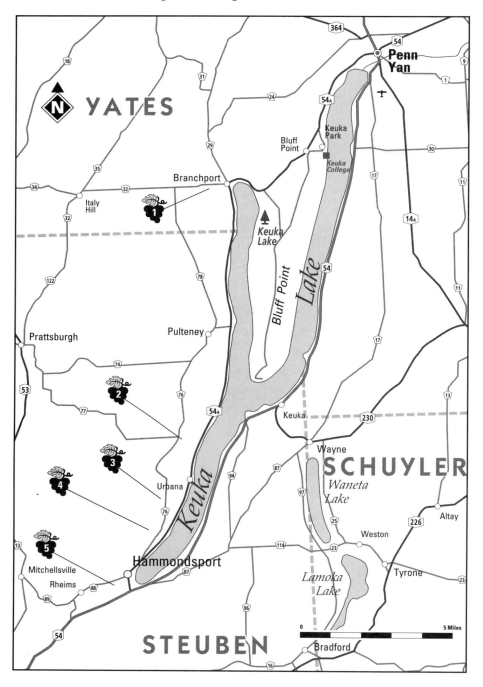

CHAPTER 3

Keuka Lake Wineries—West Side

1. Hunt Country Vineyards

Hunt Country Vineyards, 4021 Italy Hill Road, Branchport, NY14418, (315) 595-2812, www.huntcountryvineyards.com, is owned and managed by Art and Joyce Hunt. When Art and Joyce moved to the site of their winery in 1973, they became the sixth generation of Hunts to work the same soil.

Hunt Country Vineyards opened in 1988. The winery name is based on Joyce's interest in horses, and some of their wine labels show a formally dressed rider. The Hunts have taken their wines to Genesee Valley fox-hunting country near Geneseo, home of the Genesee Valley Hunt Club, and to hunt country in Virginia.

Hunt Country produces Chardonnay, aged in American oak; semi-dry Riesling; oak-aged Cabernet Franc; semi-dry Cayuga White; oak-aged Seyval Blanc; and Classic White, an oak-aged blend of Seyval Blanc and Vignoles. The winery also produces Classic Red, an oak-aged blend of Chancellor, Baco Noir, and DeChaunac; and three varieties of the popular, reasonably priced "Foxy Lady"—White, a blend of Niagara, Cayuga White, and Seyval Blanc; Blush, a blend of Delaware, Cayuga White, and Seyval Blanc; and Red, a blend of Concord, Baco Noir, DeChaunac, and Cayuga White. The winery's Hunter's Red is a blend of Chancellor, DeChaunac, Baco Noir, and Seyval Blanc, aged in stainless steel. Hunt Country Vineyards also produces brut Chardonnay Champagne, fermented in the bottle.

The focus of Hunt Country Vineyards is on specialty wines, including late harvest wines that require intensive care in the vineyard and in the wine cellar. Two of its late-harvest specialty wines are a spicy Late Harvest Vignoles and an intense Vidal Ice Wine, a dessert wine with 17 percent residual sugar. These dessert wines command a premium price because of their labor-intensive nature; the small quantity made is usually sold in half-bottles. Hunt Country also makes Cream Sherry and Ruby Port.

The building housing the tasting room dates back to the

1820s when it was a part of the large Victorian homestead. The setting is an operating farm with horses grazing near the entrance road. Hunt Country tripled the size of its tasting room in recent years and offers food to accompany its wine. The winery provides guided haywagon tours through the vineyards; picnic tables are available adjacent to the winery.

2. Dr. Frank's Vinifera Wine Cellars / Chateau Frank

Dr. Frank's Vinifera Wine Cellars, 9749 Middle Road, Hammondsport, NY 14840, www.drfrankwines.com, (607) 868-4884, produced its first vintage in 1962. Dr. Konstantin Frank proved that the finest grape varieties in the world, the European varieties of the *Vitis vinifera* specie, could be grown in the Finger Lakes Region. The winery is located six miles north of Hammondsport.

Dr. Frank's son-in-law, Walter Volz, as vineyard manager, assisted his father-in-law in planting the original Vinifera Wine Cellars vineyards. Walter and Hilda Frank Volz's son, Eric, is the vineyard manager now.

Dr. Frank, enology and viticulture pioneer, died in 1985. His son, Willy, continues the operation of Vinifera Wine Cellars. Willy's son, Fred, has been general manager and president of the winery since 1993. He is the third generation to carry on Dr. Frank's legacy.

In 1980, Willy and his wife, Margrit, purchased a 60-acre farm near Watkins Glen, where they planted over 28 acres of traditional French Champagne grape varieties: Chardonnay, Pinot Blanc, Pinot Meunier, and Pinot Noir. Willy and Margrit Frank live in a large stone house down Middle Road from the winery. Originally, the home was owned by Greyton Taylor, a son of the founder of the Taylor Wine Company, who added a wine storage facility. This facility is used for producing sparkling wine made in the *méthode champenoise* style in which the secondary fermentation providing the bubbles takes place in the bottle in which it is served.

These premium sparkling wines are marketed as Chateau

Willy and Fred Frank of Dr. Frank's Vinifera Wine Cellars

Frank Brut Champagne and Blanc de Blancs. Little of two of the four grape varieties used to make it, Pinot Blanc and Pinot Meunier, are grown in New York State. Willy refers to Pinot Meunier as the "sauce" of champagne and considers it to be a critical ingredient of a quality sparkling wine. Chateau Frank also produces sparkling Rieslings: Célèbre and Célèbre Rosé. Howard Goldberg of the New York *Times* has observed, "Chateau Frank makes sparkling wines that can rival prestigious ones from Champagne."

In addition, Dr. Frank's Vinifera Wine Cellars produces Cabernet Sauvignon, Merlot, Lemberger, barrel-fermented Chardonnay, Gewürztraminer, Pinot Gris, Cuvée Blanc, Dry Riesling, Semi-dry Riesling, and Reserve Riesling. The Wine Cellars also produces Chardonnay, Riesling, Pinot Gris, and Coho Red wines with the Salmon Run label.

The winery makes an outstanding Pinot Noir from the oldest Pinot Noir vineyards in New York State. According to *American Wine Review*, "This is Pinot Noir the way it ought to be." Susan Kroiter of the Boston *Globe* adds, "The winery is known for its Pinot Noir, one of the best red wines I've ever had." The winery also makes Fleur de Pinot Noir, a non-vintage Pinot, low in tannin, made from the fruit of young vines.

Rkatsiteli, a little-grown grape variety in the Finger Lakes Region, originated on Mt. Ararat on the border of Armenia and Turkey over 5,000 years ago. Rkatsiteli, pronounced ar-kat-si-TEL-lee, is similar to Riesling and has a touch of spiciness like Gewürztraminer.

Many wineries make their blush wines from lesser quality varieties of grapes; Vinifera Wine Cellars Première Blush is made from a blend of Chardonnay, Pinot Noir, and Riesling, added for the aroma and a touch of sweetness.

Dr. Frank's Vinifera Wine Cellars was selected as New York State Winery of the year in 2001 and has won many other awards too numerous to mention. Frank Prial of the New York *Times* observes: "Most connoisseurs agree that [Dr. Frank's] are truly extraordinary wines. They have been served at the White House and at the State House in Albany, and they have consistently beaten French wines in blind tastings." Willy Frank asks the same question that his father asked: "Why not the best?"

3. Heron Hill Winery

Heron Hill Winery, 9249 County Route 76, Hammondsport, NY 14840, (800) 441-4241, www.heronhill.com, is located three miles north of Hammondsport. Heron Hill Winery is owned by John and Josephine Ingle of Naples, New York. Their first vines were planted in 1972, and their first vintage was released in 1977. The Winery does not have a tour, but it offers winetastings from a tasting room with an outstanding view from its location high on a hillside overlooking Keuka Lake.

Heron Hill Winery produces wine from *Vitis vinifera*, French-American hybrid, and native-American grapes. Its *Vitis vinifera* wines include four Chardonnays: Ingle Vineyard Chardonnay, Chardonnay Reserve, Chardonnay, and Otter Spring Chardonnay; and four Rieslings: Dry Riesling, Semi-dry Riesling, Ingle Vineyard Riesling, and Late Harvest Riesling. The Winery also produces Ingle Vineyard Pinot Noir, Ingle Vineyard Cabernet Franc, and Eclipse, a blend of Cabernet Franc, Cabernet Sauvignon, and Merlot.

Baco Noir, Otter Spring Baco Noir, and Seyval Blanc are three of its French-American varietals. White and Red Table Wine, Game Bird White, Game Bird Red, and semi-dry Bluff Point Blush are blends made from hybrid and *Vitis vinifera* grapes. Heron Hill also produces Brut Champagne.

In 1999, Heron Hill completed a comprehensive expansion project, which includes a new tasting room, wine and retail shop, deli, conference room, banquet space, an oak barrel room, and renovations to the patio and parking areas. The expansion showcases the Winery's spectacular view of Keuka Lake and surrounding vineyards. Heron Hill has an active event and concert calendar.

4. Bully Hill Vineyards

Bully Hill Vineyards, 8843 Greyton H. Taylor Memorial Drive, Hammondsport, NY 14840, www.bullyhill.com, (607) 868-3610, is located one and a half miles north of Hammondsport, off Pulteney-Hammondsport Road (County Route 76). The winery was founded in 1970 by Walter S. Taylor, grandson of the founders of Taylor Wine Company. In 1960, Walter Taylor bought the land and buildings on Bully Hill that housed the original Taylor Wine Company, which was founded in 1880.

In addition to the winery, which specializes in French-American hybrid wines, are the popular Bully Hill Restaurant with both indoor and outdoor dining, banquet facilities, two gift shops, a wine retail store, and the Greyton H. Taylor Wine and Grape Museum. Bully Hill, which offers an informative and entertaining vineyard and winery tour followed by a winetasting, attracts over 200,000 visitors a year. The winery is the second largest in the Finger Lakes Region.

Walter Taylor was a vice president of Taylor Wine Company until 1970, when he left the company after speaking out against the large New York State wineries for using as much as 25 percent California juice in New York State wines and for ameliorating (adding water to) wine to reduce the acid content. Although these practices were legal, Taylor thought that the wine-buying public was being misled.

Taylor insisted on listing all ingredients in his Bully Hill wine. Also, he pioneered listing, on the back label of the bottle, all growers from whom he purchased grapes of a particular variety. He did not ameliorate his wine; his slogan was "Wine without water." He was against blending with California juice and spoke out against tank car wine. To illustrate his point, he purchased a railroad tank car, which stands unused outside of Bully Hill Vineyards.

In 1977, Taylor Wine Company and its parent at the time, Coca-Cola, filed a suit against Walter to prevent him from using the name "Taylor" on his Bully Hill wine labels. He

Bully Hill Vineyards

blackened out "Taylor" on his labels, which went to the wine retail stores as Walter S. XXXXXX. The classic David versus Goliath confrontation was, in terms of free publicity alone, won by Walter Taylor.

Walter Taylor made quality wine and was a talented artist. He produced many creative wine labels, motivating him to market wines with unusual names. In addition to producing varietal French-American wines, including Aurora, Baco Noir, Cayuga White, Chancellor, Chelois, Ravat (Vignoles), Seyval Blanc, Verdelet, and Vidal Blanc, Bully Hill makes many fine blends, with names such as Fishmarket White, Fusion, Happy Hen White, Love My Goat Red, Meat Market Red, Miss Love White, Space Shuttle Rosé, and Sweet Walter Red.

Bully Hill also produces blush wines, such as Le Goat Blush, Spring Blush, and Growers Blush as well as specialty wines, including Thunder Road and Wide Open to pay tribute to racing at Watkins Glen and to the National Warplane Museum at Elmira. In addition, Bully Hill produces champagne, including Mother Ship Over Paris Champagne Rouge and Seyval Blanc Brut Champagne, as well as European-style wine made from the *Vitis vinifera* specie of grapes, such as Pinot Noir and Riesling.

In May 1999, the addition of a new building increased the visitor center space to 6,500 square feet. Walter Taylor passed away in 2001. Lillian Taylor, Walter's widow, manages the winery with the able assistance of winemaker Greg Learned.

5. Pleasant Valley Wine Company
Pleasant Valley Wine Company, 8260 Pleasant Valley Road, Hammondsport, NY 14840, (607) 569-6111, is located south of Hammondsport on County Route 88. The Wine Company, maker of Great Western Champagne, was founded in 1860. As the oldest winery in the Finger Lakes Region, it was designated Bonded Winery #1. Great Western Champagne received its name in 1871, when a winetaster exclaimed,

"Truly, this will be the great champagne of the West!" His prediction became fact in 1873 when Great Western was the first champagne from the United States to win a gold prize in Europe at the Vienna Exposition.

Eight stone buildings of the Pleasant Valley Wine Company are listed in the National Register of Historic Places. The original winery carved caves deep into the hillside of Pleasant Valley for wine storage. The Visitor Center has a horseshoe-shaped, redwood-faced bar 66-foot long for winetastings; a striking stained-glass mural that depicts awards won by the company decorates the winetasting area.

Pleasant Valley Wine Company produces wine from *Vitis vinifera* grapes, such as Chardonnay and Riesling, and French-American hybrids, e.g. Verdelet, as well as native-American grapes, including Catawba, Delaware, Duchess, and Isabella. The Wine Company also produces White, Red, and Blush Table Wine blends.

The winery also makes fortified wines—Madeira, Marsala, Port, and Sherry. In addition, Pleasant Valley produces semi-dry, barrel-fermented Brut Rosé Champagne from Chardonnay and Pinot Noir grapes and Naturel, Brut, and Extra-Dry Champagne from predominately Chardonnay grapes, as well as Spumante, Sparkling Burgundy, and Special Reserve Sparkling Wine, made from 100% Riesling.

The Visitor Center has a comprehensive wine museum with a display of barrels and casks, coopers' equipment and tools used in the 1800s, and a working model of the Bath-Hammondsport Railroad as it was in the "old days." The model of the old "Champagne Trail" railroad, which has 168 feet of track and 28 switches, was built by the Niagara-Orleans Model Engineers Club of Lockport, New York, over a two-year period. The Wine Company's modern bottling facility is adjacent to the museum. The Visitor Center has an extensive wine and gift shop.

In 2002, Pleasant Valley Wine Company established a retail store at 2 Franklin Street, Watkins Glen, NY 14891.

Pleasant Valley Wine Company

Keuka Lake, Looking East

CHAPTER 4

Keuka Lake Wineries—East Side

"With years a richer life begins,
    The spirit mellows:
Ripe age gives tone to violins,
    Wine, and good fellows."

John Townsend Trowbridge, *Three Worlds*

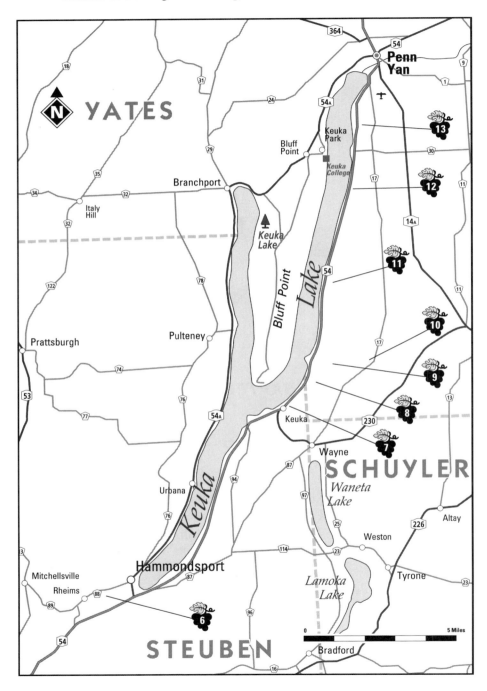

CHAPTER 4

Keuka Lake Wineries—East Side

6. Chateau Renaissance Wine Cellars

Chateau Renaissance Wine Cellars, 7494 Hatchery Road, Bath, NY 14810, www.chateaurenaissance.com, (607) 569-3609, is located on a rustic road halfway between Hammondsport and Bath, just south of the Pleasant Valley Inn. The 3,200-square-foot winery was founded in 2001 by Domenic Carisetti and Patrice Demay. Domenic Carisetti's winemaking background was principally at Taylor / Great Western. Patrice Demay is from a winemaking family who owned five wineries in France.

The winery produces a bone-dry Chardonnay, mellow Don Nuncio made mainly with Steuben grapes, and sweet D'Artagnan with Niagara grapes. Blends include Aramis, a semi-dry, Riesling-like blend of native grape varieties; Athos, a red blend of French-American hybrid and *Vitis vinifera* varieties; and semi-dry Royal Blush.

Chateau Renaissance also produces champagne, including dry Brut; medium-dry Demi-Sec, a blend of Riesling and Seyval Blanc; medium-sweet Doux; and Rouge, a blend of Merlot, DeChaunac, and Concord; in addition to Apple, Blackberry, Peach, and Raspberry sparkling wines. The winery also makes Cherry, Cranberry, Peach, Pear, Strawberry Rhubarb fruit wines, as well as dandelion wine.

7. Ravines Wine Cellars

Ravines Wine Cellars, 14110 Route 54, Hammondsport, NY 14840, (607) 292-7007, is located in Keuka Village, near the Switzerland Inn. The winery, established in 2003, is owned and managed by Lisa and Morten Hallgren, who is also the winemaker. Morten grew up with his family's vineyard and winery in southern France. He has degrees in enology and viticulture from L'Ecole Agronomie Superior, one of the top winemaking schools in France.

Ravines Wine Cellars produces Chardonnay, Riesling, Pinot Noir, and Meritage Blend, a blend of Cabernet Sauvignon and Cabernet Franc, as well as Finger Lakes

White, a Cayuga White / Vignoles blend. The Provençal-inspired tasting room has a gourmet shop. The winery is "picnic-friendly" and handicapped accessible.

8. Fall Bright, the Winemakers Shoppe

Fall Bright, the Winemakers Shoppe, 9750 Hyatt Hill, Wayne, NY 14893, (607) 292-3995, is located nine miles north of Hammondsport, off East Lake Road (Route 54). The juice plant and winemakers supply shop overlooks the eastern shore of Keuka Lake. Fall Bright produces 30 varieties of grapes and pressed juice for amateur winemakers.

Most of Fall Bright's customers are from western New York, but some are from as far away as Connecticut, New Hampshire, New Jersey, and Pennsylvania. Fall Bright can press over four tons of grapes an hour and has a large refrigerated cooler capacity to store grapes and juice until picked up by customers. Fall Bright stocks books on grapegrowing and winemaking and a full line of winemaking and beermaking supplies.

9. McGregor Vineyard & Winery

McGregor Vineyard & Winery, 5503 Dutch Street, Dundee, NY 14837, (607) 292-3999, www.mcgregorwinery.com, is located nine miles north of Hammondsport, off East Lake Road (Route 54). Founders Bob and Marge McGregor planted their first grapevines in 1971 and produced their first commercial wines in 1980. Their son, John, and daughter-in-law, Stacey, manage the vineyard and premium estate winery.

McGregor specializes in *Vitis vinifera* wines, including four Chardonnays: Chardonnay Reserve, aged in French oak; Chardonnay Barrel Fermente; a clean, crisp Unoaked Chardonnay; and Semi-dry Chardonnay. The Winery also makes five Rieslings: Dry (Alsatian style), Semi-dry, Semi-sweet, Bunch Select, and Sparkling Riesling, as well as Gewürztraminer and Gewürztraminer Reserve.

In addition, McGregor produces medium-bodied Pinot

Noir, aged in French oak; Pinot Noir Reserve, made from a Gamay Beaujolais clone; medium-bodied Cabernet Franc; Rosé d'Cabernet Franc; semi-dry Muscat Ottonel; and Muscat Ottonel Reserve. The Winery also produces Blanc de Noir from Pinot Noir, a fermented-in-the-bottle sparkling wine; and a 100% Chardonnay Blanc de Blancs.

McGregor blends include Black Russian, a full-bodied red blend of Saperavi, which is a Russian blending grape, and Sereksiya; White Russian, a Sereksiya Rosé / Rkatsiteli blend; Rob Roy, a blend of Cabernet Franc, Cabernet Sauvignon, and Merlot, aged in French oak; oak-aged Highlands Red, a semi-dry blend of French-American hybrid grapes; and Sunflower White, a blend of Cayuga, Riesling, Chardonnay, Sereksiya Rosé, Rkatsiteli, and Vignoles.

The McGregors have provided a large deck from which to view Keuka Lake while sipping their fine wines.

10. Keuka Overlook Wine Cellars

Keuka Overlook Wine Cellars, 5777 Old Bath Road, Dundee, NY 14837, (607) 292-6877, www.keukaoverlook.com, was established in 1993 by Bob and Terry Barrett. The winery has a panoramic view of Keuka Lake.

Keuka Overlook produces three Chardonnays: Chardonnay with 2% residual sugar, barrel-aged Blue Lake Chardonnay, and Chardonnay Reserve, which is fermented in French and American oak, as well as Cabernet Sauvignon, Cabernet Franc, Pinot Noir, Merlot, Johannisberg Riesling, and Alsatian-style Gewürztraminer. The winery also produces blends, including Triumph, a blend of Cabernet Sauvignon, Cabernet Franc, and Merlot; Victorian Red, a blend of Baco Noir, Rougeon, and Chambourcin; and Victorian Rosé, a blend of Gewürztraminer, Riesling, Cayuga, Seyval Blanc, and Colobel. In addition, it produces semi-dry Rougeon, a French-American hybrid red; and Blueberry, Red Raspberry, and Riesling dessert wines, as well as Blueberry, Cherry, and Mulberry sparkling wines.

Keuka Overlook Wine Cellars has a picnic area and a gift shop. It is adjacent to Keuka Overlook Bed & Breakfast Inn.

11. Barrington Cellars

Barrington Cellars, 2772 Gray Road, Penn Yan, NY 14527, (315) 536-9686, www.barringtoncellars.com, was established by Ken and Eileen Farnan in 1971. Barrington Cellars is housed in a 100-year-old farmhouse / wine shop east of Keuka Lake, off Route 54.

Barrington Cellars *Vitis vinifera* wines include oak-aged Chardonnay, Semi-dry Gewürztraminer, Semi-dry Riesling, and Pinot Noir. Barrington Cellars also makes wine from native-American grapes, including Catawba, Delaware, Diamond, and Isabella, as well as French-American hybrid grapes, such as Baco Noir, DeChaunac, Seyval Blanc, and Vidal Blanc. The winery also produces Buzzard's Peach, a fruit wine; and dessert ice wines, including Niagara, Isabella, and Bliss, a Vidal Blanc / Delaware blend.

12. Rooster Hill Vineyards

Rooster Hill Vineyards, 489 Route 54, Penn Yan, NY 14527, (315) 536-4773, www.roosterhill.com, is located five miles south of Penn Yan. The winery, which is owned and managed by David and Amy Hoffman, opened in 2003.

The Hoffmans have planted Cabernet Franc, Riesling, Pinot Noir, and Lemberger vines in their Savina Estate Vineyard and the same varieties plus Gewürztraminer in their Catherine Estate Vineyard at a slightly higher elevation. Initially, they are buying high-quality grapes from premium growers in the Finger Lakes region and Long Island.

The winery's *Vitis vinifera* wines are Merlot, Cabernet Sauvignon, Cabernet Franc, Pinot Noir, and Riesling. Some of Rooster Hill's wine is aged in French and American oak barrels. It also produces Seyval Blanc, Cayuga White, Vidal Blanc, and Silver Pencil, a proprietary white blend. The wine-tasting room is decorated in Tuscan style.

13. Keuka Spring Vineyards

Keuka Spring Vineyards, 272 East Lake Road (Route 54), Penn Yan, NY 14527, www.keukaspringwinery.com, (315) 536-3147, is located three miles south of Penn Yan in a historic setting with an 1840s homestead and a gambrel-roofed barn housing a rustic winetasting room. Keuka Spring owners Judy and Len Wiltberger planted their first vines in 1981 and produced their first wine in 1985.

The winery's European white varietals include barrel-aged Chardonnay, Semi-dry Riesling, and Gewürztraminer. French-American hybrid whites include dry Seyval Blanc, semi-sweet Cayuga White, and Vignoles.

Keuka Spring also produces wine from the European red grape varieties Cabernet Franc, Cabernet Sauvignon, Lemberger, Merlot, and Pinot Noir. Blends include hearty Crooked Lake Red, a blend of Baco Noir and Maréchal Foch; semi-dry Celebrate!, a Riesling / Seyval Blanc blend; and Epic, a meritage blend of Cabernet Franc, Cabernet Sauvignon, and Merlot. Other Keuka Spring wines include Harvest Blush and Clara's Red. Picnic tables are provided on winery grounds.

Keuka Lake Wine Trail

Eight wineries participate in the Keuka Lake Wine Trail, 2375 Route 14A, Penn Yan, NY 14527, (800) 440-4898:
- Barrington Cellars
- Chateau Renaissance Wine Cellars
- Dr. Frank's Vinifera Wine Cellars / Chateau Frank
- Heron Hill Winery
- Hunt Country Vineyards
- Keuka Overlook Wine Cellars
- Keuka Spring Vineyards
- McGregor Vineyard & Winery

The Wine Trail plans about five joint activities a year. The Wine Trail's website is: www.keukawinetrail.com.

CHAPTER 5

Seneca Lake Wineries—West Side

"Wine: An infallible antidote to common sense and seriousness; an excuse for deeds otherwise unforgivable."

Elbert Hubbard, *The Roycroft Dictionary and Book of Epigrams*, 1923.

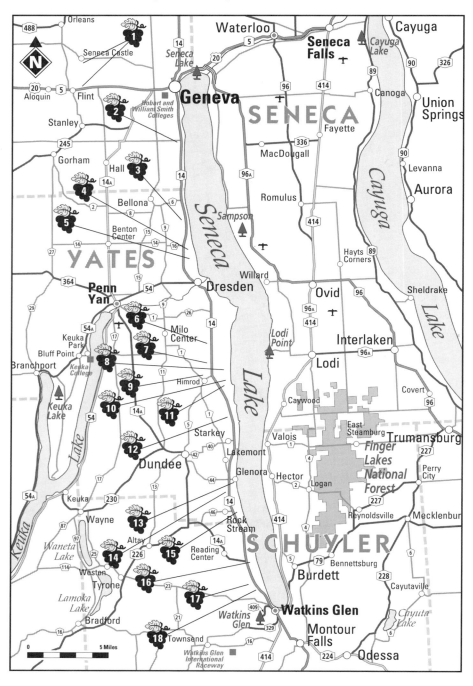

CHAPTER 5

Seneca Lake Wineries—West Side

1. Amberg Wine Cellars

Amberg Wine Cellars retail store, 2200 Routes 5 & 20, Flint, NY 14561, (585) 526-6742, www.ambergwine.com, is located west of Geneva. The winery is owned by Herman and Ute Amberg, who have supplied grapevines to area growers for over 30 years as the Amberg Grafted Grape Vine Nursery.

The original winery, founded in 1990, was located in Seneca Castle in the barns of a farm established in 1795. The winery burned down in 1996 and was rebuilt in 1997.

Amberg Wine Cellars produces oak-aged Chardonnay Barrel Select, barrel-aged Semi-dry Chardonnay, Dry Riesling, Semi-dry Riesling, Pinot Noir, full-bodied Cabernet Sauvignon, Burgundy, and Bordeaux-style Claret. The winery is one of the few in the region that produces Traminette, a hybrid of Gewürztraminer.

Amberg's blends include crisp, clean Blanc; semi-dry Pearl; and semi-sweet Gypsy, blends of Traminette and Riesling; semi-dry Red Panda, a Cabernet Franc / Merlot blend; and semi-sweet Red Baron. The winery also produces Blush; Bianca, a Hungarian grape variety similar to Sauvignon Blanc and Chardonnay; and two sweet wines: Pegasus and Mandolin, a blend of Siegfried, Riesling, and Muscat.

Winemaker Eric Amberg acquired his winemaking expertise at wineries in California, Germany, and New York State after earning a degree in enology at Fresno State University in California.

2. Billsboro Estates Winery

Billsboro Estates Winery, 4760 Route 14, Geneva, NY 14456, (315) 789-9538, produces *Vitis vinifera* varietal wines and blends. The Winery, which is owned by Dr. Robert Pool of the New York State Agricultural Experiment Station and Jennifer Morris, opened in 2000.

Billsboro Estates produces Chardonnay, Cabernet Franc, and Pinot Noir. The Winery's blends include Bordeaux-style

Red Eclectsia, a blend of Cabernet Franc, Syrah, Sangiovese, and Barbera; White Eclectsia, a blend of Chenin Blanc, Sauvignon Blanc, Viognier, Rkatsiteli, and Pinot Gris; and Eclectsia Blush, fermented with a Sherry yeast. The Winery also produces a late harvest Delaware dessert wine.

3. Fox Run Vineyards

Fox Run Vineyards, 670 Route 14, Penn Yan, NY 14527, (315) 536-4616, www.foxrunvineyards.com, is located eight miles south of Geneva. Scott Osborn is the owner and president. Peter Bell is the winemaker. The winery, which has over 50 acres of vineyards, is located on a 150-acre farm with a Victorian-style house that has natural mahogany, cherry, and chestnut woodwork, and a circa 1860s barn.

Fox Run specializes in *Vitis vinifera* wine, including Cabernet Sauvignon, Merlot, Pinot Noir, Cabernet Franc, and Lemberger, as well as Chardonnay, barrel-aged Reserve Chardonnay, Dry Riesling, Semi-dry Riesling, and Gewürztraminer. It also makes Ruby Vixen, a semi-dry blush blend of Cayuga White, Chardonnay, Riesling, and Vincent; Arctic Fox, a crisp blend of Cayuga White, Chardonnay, and Riesling; Sable, a blend of Cabernet Sauvignon, Merlot, and Cabernet Franc with oak flavors; and Meritage, an oak-aged blend of Merlot, Cabernet Franc, and Cabernet Sauvignon.

The winery has an award-winning café and an extensive gift shop. Fox Run offers a comprehensive winery tour that includes Fox Run's state of the art processing facility, a stroll through the vineyard to learn about grapegrowing, and a visit to the barrel room for a tasting.

4. Seneca Shore Wine Cellars

Seneca Shore Wine Cellars, 929 Davy Road (off Route 14), Penn Yan, NY 14527, (315) 536-0882, is owned and managed by David DeMarco. The winery produces "medieval wines of the Finger Lakes." The motif of the winetasting room is a medieval castle with simulated torches on the walls, upon

Fox Run Vineyards

which are hung weapons of the Middle Ages, such as battle axes and maces. The personable, knowledgeable women conducting the winetastings have been known to dress in medieval costumes.

Seneca Shore's wine labels were designed by highly regarded Rochester artist Martha Sweeney. Depicted on the labels is a goddess in the heavens blowing down on a sailing ship being propelled toward a medieval city. One is reminded of the parting wish "may the wind always be at your back."

Seneca Shore Wine Cellars dry white wines include Gewürztraminer; Chardonnay-Smooth; Chardonnay, aged in stainless steel; Dry Riesling; Semi-dry Riesling; Vinho Grigio; and White Castle, made from Cayuga White. The winery's dry red wines include Cabernet Franc, Cabernet Sauvignon, Merlot, Pinot Noir, Pinot Noir-Balanced Barrel, Lemberger, Red Knight, and Red Castle, made from Baco Noir.

Seneca Shore also produces semi-dry Moon Rise, semi-sweet Royal White, and Royal Rosé. In addition, the winery makes sweet wines, such as Royal Nectar, Castle Blush, Royal Red, and Red Sail, a blend of DeChaunac and Cayuga. Seneca Shore has an open deck with rocking chairs and a covered deck overlooking Seneca Lake.

5. Anthony Road Wine Company

Anthony Road Wine Company, 1225 Anthony Road (off Route 14) Penn Yan, NY 14527, www.anthonyroadwine.com, (315) 536-2182, is located 10 miles south of Geneva. The winery, established in 1989, is owned by John and Ann Martini. The Wine Company opened an attractive new winetasting facility in 1998.

Anthony Road Wine Company produces Dry Riesling, Semi-dry Riesling, Pinot Gris, Cabernet Franc, and a blend of oak-fermented and stainless-steel-fermented Chardonnay. The winery's French-American hybrid wines include Seyval Blanc and Dry and Semi-dry Vignoles as well as Late Harvest

Vignoles dessert wine. The Wine Company also produces blends such as semi-sweet Poulet Rouge, a blend of Cayuga and Rougeon; semi-sweet Tony's Red, a blend of Rougeon, Baco Noir, and Vignoles; semi-sweet Solstice, a blend of Chardonnay and Cayuga; dry Vintner's Red, a Baco Noir / Rougeon blend; and 1.5 liter Vintner's Select, a blend of Seyval Blanc, Cayuga White, Chardonnay, and Vignoles.

In 2001, winemaker Robert Young of California's Alexander Valley purchased 105 acres of vineyard land north of Dresden. Young is partnering with Anthony Road Wine Company. John and Ann Martini's son, Peter, made the initial plantings of Pinot Gris, Chardonnay, Merlot, and Gewürztraminer vines in Young's vineyard.

6. Prejean Winery

Prejean Winery, 2634 Route 14, Penn Yan, NY 14527, (315) 536-7524, www.prejeanwinery.com, was established in 1985. Elizabeth Prejean and her son, Tom, manage the winery and over 30 acres of vineyards. The Winery produces stainless-steel-fermented Chardonnay; Vintner's Reserve Chardonnay, fermented in French oak and aged sur lies; Dry and Semi-dry Riesling; Dry and Semi-dry Gewürztraminer; Cabernet Sauvignon; Cabernet Franc; and Merlot *Vitis vinifera* wine, as well as Maréchal Foch and semi-sweet Cayuga White wine from French-American hybrid grapes.

Prejean blends include dry Proprietor's Red, a blend of Maréchal Foch, Cayuga, and Riesling; and semi-sweet Tiger Lily, a blend of Maréchal Foch, Cayuga White, Riesling, and Chardonnay. The Winery also makes Late Harvest Vignoles and Late Harvest Chardonnay dessert wine.

Prejean Winery is increasing its plantings of red grapevines and has added Bird of Paradise Port, made with Chardonnay, to their offerings. Their 6,000-square-foot facility, which provides a beautiful view of Seneca Lake, accommodates the crushing, pressing, aging, warehousing, tasting, and retailing needs of the Winery.

7. *Torrey Ridge Winery*

Torrey Ridge Winery, 2770 Route 14, Penn Yan, NY, (315) 536-1210, www.torreyridgewinery.com, opened in 1999. The Winery has winetasting rooms on the first and second floors. The second-floor winetasting room, which has a small balcony, provides a panoramic view of Seneca Lake.

Torrey Ridge produces wine from European grape varieties, such as Chardonnay and Riesling, in addition to French-American hybrids Cayuga White, Seyval Blanc, Rosette, Rougeon, and Baco Noir, as well as native-American varieties, including Catawba, Diamond, and Niagara. The Winery's Blue Sapphire is made from 100% Concord grapes. It also makes semi-sweet wines: Bandit Red from Baco Noir and Allusive from Seyval Blanc.

Examples of the Winery's blends are Torrey Ridge Red, a blend of Rougeon, Baco Noir, and Maréchal Foch; Summit, a Pinot Noir / Baco Noir blend; Heritage, a blend of Rougeon, Maréchal Foch, Chancellor, and Vincent; Bandit Blush, made from Concord and Rougeon; Torrey Ridge Blush, a Rougeon / Niagara blend; and Indigo Blush made from Concord and Honey Mead. Torrey Ridge's specialty wines include semi-sweet Peach Wine; semi-sweet Summer Delight, made from strawberry, rhubarb, and honey wine; Scarlet Red, a dessert wine blend of raspberry, cranberry, and honey wine; and Ruby Red, a cherry wine / honey wine blend.

Torrey Ridge Winery offers educational tours of their winery and honey production facility. Visitors are welcome to walk around the vineyards.

8. *Miles Wine Cellars*

Miles Wine Cellars, 168 Randall Crossing Road (off Route 14), Himrod, NY 14842, www.mileswinecellars.com, (607) 243-7742, is owned and managed by Doug and Suzy Hayes Miles. The winetasting room is located in a beautiful, over-200-year-old Greek Revival mansion that Doug spent more than 17 years restoring. He planted his first grapevines in

Miles Wine Cellars

1978 and now has over 60 acres under cultivation.

The Miles Wine Cellars winemaker is Peter Bell, one of the top Finger Lakes winemakers. The mansion, located on the western shoreline of Seneca Lake, has a dock, allowing visitors to come by boat.

Miles Wine Cellars *Vitis vinifera* wines include Cabernet Franc, barrel fermented in Hungarian oak; Pinot Noir, barrel fermented in French oak; and Semi-dry Riesling, fermented in stainless steel. The winery also produces semi-dry Cayuga White.

Miles Wine Cellars blends include Milestone, a blend of Merlot and Cabernet Franc; and semi-sweet Wisteria, a Catawba / Ives blend.

9. Earle Estates Winery & Meadery

Earle Estates Winery & Meadery, 3586 Route 14, Himrod, NY 14842, (315) 536-1210, www.meadery.com, is owned by John and Esthee Earle. Earle Estates produces over 30 honey wines (mead) and fruit wines. The Earle Estates literature describes the history of mead:

> Mead dates back through antiquity with Nordic legends and non-mythological history in Greek, Hindu, Roman, and British cultures. Once considered a divine beverage, mead was thought to be the giver of life, with a common belief that it fell from heaven as dew, then was collected by the honeybee from flowers. This placed honey, the bee, and mead in high stature in sacred mythology.

Earle Estates, which also owns Torrey Ridge Winery, produces Riesling and lightly oaked Chardonnay, as well as dry Seyval Blanc and semi-dry Cayuga White. The Winery also makes wine from the native-American grape variety Diamond and produces blends, such as Cardinal Red, a blend of DeChaunac, Maréchal Foch, and Chancellor; and Starlight Blush, a Diamond / Rougeon blend. It also makes 100% fruit wines, including semi-dry Pear wine and Crimson Blush, an apple / cranberry fruit wine.

The Meadery produces Honey Mead Contemporary Dry, Honey Mead Semi-sweet, and Honey Mead Traditional from two different processes, as well as many fruit wine / mead blends, including:
- Apple Cyser—apple wine and honey mead
- Black Jewel—black raspberry wine and honey mead
- Blueberry Bounty—blueberry wine and honey mead
- Candlelight Blush—Concord grape wine and honey mead
- Cherry Charisma—cherry wine and honey mead
- Creamy Apricot—apricot wine and honey mead
- Cruisin' Cranberry—cranberry wine and honey mead
- Raspberry Reflections—red raspberry wine and honey mead
- Strawberry Shadows—strawberry wine and honey mead

10. Four Chimneys Farm Winery
Four Chimneys Farm Winery, 211 Hall Road (off Route 14), Himrod, NY 14842, www.fourchimneysorganicwines.com, (607) 243-7502, located 15 miles north of Watkins Glen, was established in 1980. The property includes an Italianate chateau with four chimneys and a Victorian barn. Four Chimneys was the first organic winery in the region.

Four Chimneys Farm Winery's goals in organic viticulture are to spare wine drinkers from harmful residuals in the wine from chemicals used in the vineyard and to safeguard the environment. A cover crop of clover is used between rows of grapevines as a source of nitrogen. Most vineyardists add only two ingredients to the soil, usually nitrogen for the vines and potash for the grapes; Four Chimneys Winery adds about 20 natural elements, including boron and manganese, to balance the soil and enhance the vigor of the vines.

Four Chimneys also takes an organic approach to wine-making by using an extensive, progressive filtration system to prevent spoilage by refermentation of the cold-stabilized finished wine. The Winery produces dry, oak-fermented Reserve White, which is predominately Chardonnay; dry, mildly oaked Kingdom White, made in the style of white Bordeaux; Eye of the Dove, a light-bodied red; dry Kingdom Red, similar to Merlot; and full-bodied, lightly oaked Reserve Red, made with Cabernet Franc.

The Winery also makes semi-dry white Dayspring; semi-sweet Eye of the Bee, made from Concord grapes and honey; and semi-sweet Golden Crown, a blush made from Catawba, Delaware, and Niagara. Four Chimneys sweet wines include Kyrie, a late harvest dessert wine made in the style of Sauterne; and Shingle Point Red, a Port-style wine with 14% alcohol.

Four Chimneys also produces brut Coronation, an organic champagne made by the traditional fermented-in-the-bottle *méthode champenoise*. The Winery's fruit wines include Dry Blueberry, semi-sweet Honeydew Moon, and sweet wines: Celestial Peach, Blueberry Skies, Strawberry Meadows, Raspberry Sunrise, and Wild Blue Yonder, made from 100% wild blueberries.

11. Woodbury Vineyards

Woodbury Vineyards, located at 4141 Route 14, Dundee, NY 14837, (607) 243-8925, www.noblevintages.com, is the Finger Lakes retail store for the parent Woodbury Vineyards in Fredonia, Chautauqua County, on Lake Erie. The winery produces five wines aged in American oak: Chardonnay; Cabernet Sauvignon; Cabernet Franc; Merlot, blended with Cabernet Sauvignon; and Glacier Ridge Red, a Baco Noir / Cabernet Franc blend; as well as Semi-dry Riesling and Alsatian-style Dry Riesling.

The winery also makes Seyval Blanc; semi-sweet Niagara; Seaport White, a Seyval Blanc / Cayuga White blend; semi-sweet White Seaport Red, a blend of Maréchal Foch and DeChaunac; and Seaport Blush, similar to white Zinfandel; as well as three semi-sweet blends: White Renard, a blend of Niagara and Cayuga White; Blush Renard, a Niagara / Concord blend; and Red Renard, made from Concord grapes.

Woodbury Vineyards also makes sweet Strawberry Wine; Cherry Wine, a sweet dessert wine; and Vidal Ice Wine, a late-harvest dessert wine. The winery has picnic tables and a deck that provides a great view of Seneca Lake.

12. Hermann J. Wiemer Vineyard

Hermann J. Wiemer Vineyard, 3962 Route 14, Dundee, NY 14837, (607) 243-7971, www.wiemer.com, is located 14 miles north of Watkins Glen. Hermann Wiemer, whose family has been in the wine industry in the Mosel Valley in Germany for over 300 years, immigrated to the United States in 1968. He was raised in Bernkastel, where his father managed the agricultural experiment station, and received his education in the Rheinpfalz and Rheingau districts of Germany.

From 1968 to 1980, Wiemer was the winemaker for Walter Taylor at Bully Hill Vineyards, which specializes in French-American hybrid wines. Wiemer's ambition was to work with *Vitis vinifera* grapes. In 1973, he purchased 140 acres of land overlooking Seneca Lake and started by planting 10 acres with hand-grafted vines. By 1992, the vineyard had stabilized at 50 acres under cultivation in that location.

The winery makes wine only from *Vitis vinifera* grapes, the world's premier varieties. Its white wines include dry, full-bodied Chardonnay, fermented in French oak; a Mosel-style Dry Riesling; Spätlese-style Semi-dry Riesling; Alsatian-style Late Harvest Riesling; Select Late Harvest Riesling, which is pressed from grapes affected by botrytis mold ("noble rot"); and a medium-dry Gewürztraminer. The winery also makes two full-bodied champagnes using the

Méthode Champenoise: Cuvée Brut, a smooth, dry cuvée made with Pinot Noir and Chardonnay grapes; and dry Blanc de Blancs, which is less austere than Cuvée Brut.

Hermann J. Wiemer Vineyard also produces Pinot Noir, aged in French oak; and Merlot (comparable to a French Pomerol) made with grapes from vines grafted and grown for a year in Wiemer vineyards and planted in Monterey, California. Harvested grapes are shipped to the Wiemer winery for production of the wine. The winery also produces a Select Late Harvest Ice Wine, residual sugar 17.5%, made from hand-selected frozen grapes from 30-year-old vines.

Wiemer Vineyard's blends include lightly oaked Estate White, made from Riesling, Chardonnay, and Pinot Gris grapes; full-bodied Dry Rosé, a Pinot Noir / Gamay blend; and Estate Red, made from Pinot Noir, Gamay, and Dornfelder, a German cross of two varieties known for depth of color.

Wiemer also operates a successful vine nursery operation, one of the largest in the United States, with production that averages 200,000 plants annually. *Vitis vinifera* vines are less winter hardy and more susceptible to the Phylloxera root louse than other varieties, such as native-American and French-American hybrid vines; therefore, they are grafted onto hardy root stock.

13. Glenora Wine Cellars

Glenora Wine Cellars, 5435 Route 14, Dundee, NY 14837, (607) 243-5511, www.glenora.com, is located eight miles north of Watkins Glen. Gene Pierce is the CEO of Glenora Wine Cellars. The winery, established in 1977, specializes in European grape varieties, such as Chardonnay, Riesling, Cabernet Sauvignon, and Merlot. The winery has been making sparkling Blanc de Blancs since 1981.

Glenora produces Chardonnay, aged in French oak barrels; lightly oaked Barrel Fermented Chardonnay; Dry Riesling; semi-sweet Riesling; Gewürztraminer; lightly oaked Barrel Fermented Pinot Blanc; as well as Cabernet Sauvignon, Syrah, and three red wines aged in French oak: Vintner's Select Pinot Noir, Vintner's Select Cabernet Franc, and Vintner's Select Merlot.

The winery also makes semi-dry Seyval Blanc, semi-dry Baco Noir Rosé, semi-sweet Cayuga White, and semi-sweet Classic Blush, which is similar to White Zinfandel. Its blends include Alpine White, Classic Red, Bobsled Red, and Jammin' Red, a blend of wine and natural fruit flavor.

Glenora Wine Cellars also produces semi-sweet Catawba, semi-sweet Niagara, and four sweet fruit wines: Cranberry Chablis, Blueberry Breeze, Raspberry Rosé, and Peach Passion, as well as two semi-sweet sparkling wines: Spumante and Peach Spumante, fermented in the bottle. Glenora's sparkling wines include Blanc de Blancs, made from 100% Chardonnay; and Brut, a blend of Pinot Noir and Chardonnay.

Glenora takes advantage of the viticultural diversity of New York State by using grapes from vineyards on three of the Finger Lakes and from North Fork on Long Island. Some of the grapes used to make Glenora's Cabernet Sauvignon and Merlot wines are from Long Island, which has a slightly longer growing season than the Finger Lakes Region. French winemakers blend Merlot and small percentages of other varieties, such as Malbec, with Cabernet Sauvignon to make Bordeaux mellower. Glenora also uses Chardonnay grapes from Long Island in some of its wines and trucks in grapes from California in the fall.

Glenora Wine Cellars does not offer a winery tour, but it shows a well-produced video of its winery operations. During the summer and fall, Glenora sponsors live music on the grounds of the winery. In 1999, The Inn at Glenora Wine Cellars opened with 30 rooms for lodging, a conference center, and a restaurant, "Veraisons," accommodating 150 with a spectacular view of Seneca Lake. Ten of the rooms at the Inn have Jacuzzis and fireplaces. All of the rooms have a lake

Glenora Wine Cellars

view and a deck. The $3.5 million renovation added 33,000 square feet to the winery complex, including additional retail sales space.

14. Fulkerson Winery and Juice Plant

Fulkerson Winery and Juice Plant, 5576 Route 14, Dundee, NY 14837, (607) 243-7883, eight miles north of Watkins Glen, is owned and managed by Sayre and Nancy Fulkerson. The Fulkersons are the sixth generation to live on property that has been a family farm since 1805. Their juice plant has sold quality grape juice and winemaking supplies to home winemakers for more than 30 years. Fulkerson Winery offers over 30 varieties of fresh, premium Finger Lakes grapes and juice during the harvest season, from late August / early September through October.

Grapes are picked when the sugar content reaches acceptable levels; about 22 percent is the optimum. The timing of picking varies by grape variety. The French-American hybrid white, Aurora, is usually picked during Labor Day week, and another hybrid white, Vidal Blanc, is picked in late October, sometimes in Indian-summer conditions.

Fulkerson Winery, which opened in 1990, produces barrel-fermented and oak-aged Chardonnay; Gewürztraminer; Dry Riesling; semi-sweet Johannisberg Riesling; full-bodied Cabernet Sauvignon; Pinot Noir, aged in French oak; Merlot; and light-bodied Cabernet Franc. The Winery also makes Ravat (Vignoles); Traminette, a hybrid of Gewürztraminer with some of the spicy taste; Diamond; and Vincent.

The Winery's blends include Reserve Red, a blend of Cabernet Franc, Baco Noir, and Chelois; semi-sweet Bridge White, a blend of Cayuga White, Seyval Blanc, Riesling, and Gewürztraminer; Bridge Red, a blend of Baco Noir, Chelois, Aurora, and Lakemont; and three sweet wines: Sunset Blush, made with Catawba grapes; Red Zeppelin, a popular Catawba / Rougeon blend; and Matinee. Fulkerson Winery also produces award-winning Vidal Ice Wine.

15. Arcadian Estate Vineyards

Arcadian Estate Vineyards, 4184 Route 14, Rock Stream, NY 14878, (607) 535-2068, www.arcadianwine.com, is housed in a three-story, 170-year-old barn with a gourmet cheese and meat court in an all-natural hardwood winetasting room. Arcadian Estate Vineyards has an art gallery and claims to have a 130-year-old ghost who "is often available to greet visitors." The winery specializes in red wine and fruit wine.

Arcadian Estate Vineyards produces "Two Roads" Chardonnay, medium-bodied "White Series" Pinot Noir, and "Silver Series" Pinot Noir. Its blends include Sail Away, a Chardonnay / Cayuga White blend; semi-dry Watkins White; semi-dry Watkins "way cool" Blush; and semi-dry Watkins Red, which is predominately Rougeon.

Arcadian Estates speciality wines include "Phantom" Sherry, "Phantom" Port, and semi-dry "White Rose" Blush Champagne. The winery also makes "Shining on me" Pear, Cherry Fantasy, "Take My Time" Black Raspberry, and Strawberry fruit wines, as well as sweet Dandelion Wine.

16. Lakewood Vineyards Winery

Lakewood Vineyards Winery, 4024 Route 14, Watkins Glen, NY 14891, (607) 535-9252, www.lakewoodvineyards.com, six miles north of Watkins Glen, was established in 1988. Lakewood Vineyards makes wine from native-American, French-American hybrid, and *Vitis vinifera* grapes. The Stamp family has grown quality wine grapes for generations, beginning when Charles Stamp planted grapevines near Reading Center in 1918.

By the late 1980s, Lakewood Vineyards Winery had 52 acres of grapevines under cultivation, after adding Chardonnay, Pinot Noir, Riesling, Cayuga White, and Vignoles vines to the original Catawba and Concord. It now has over 65 acres of vineyards.

Lakewood produces Chardonnay, Dry Riesling, Semi-dry Riesling, medium-bodied Cabernet Franc, Pinot Noir,

Lakewood Vineyards Winery

Reserve Pinot Noir, and Crystallus, a meritage Cabernet Sauvignon / Cabernet Franc blend. The Winery's other blends include Long Stem Red, a blend of Baco Noir, Chancellor, Maréchal Foch, and Leon Millot; Long Stem White, a Cayuga White / Vidal Blanc blend; and Abby Rosé, made principally with Concord and Delaware.

The Winery also produces four semi-sweet wines: Vignoles, Delaware, White Catawba, and Niagara, and two ice wines: Borealis, made from Niagara; and Glaciovinum, made from Delaware; as well as Port, made from Baco Noir.

Lakewood Vineyards Winery is a family operation from winemaking to retail sales. The Winery can easily be identified by rows of rosebushes planted along Route 14, parallel to their vineyard rows. The logo of Lakewood Vineyards, the rose, appears on their brochures, labels, newsletters, and signs.

17. Cascata Winery at the Professors' Inn

Cascata Winery at the Professors' Inn, 3651 Route 14, Watkins Glen, NY 14891, www.cascatawinery.com, (607) 535-8000, is located two miles north of Watkins Glen. The Professors' Bed and Breakfast, situated in a 1800s historic house, provides winetastings and food. Wine gifts, old books, and regional art works, which are for sale, provide the décor. The house is surrounded by a porch; a garden patio and a shaded picnic area with a fish pond and stream are located nearby, along with a shed that houses an art studio and gallery.

The Winery features the Professors' Classics: dry Reserve Riesling; semi-dry Cascade Riesling; Reserve Chardonnay, aged in French oak; oak-aged Reserve Pinot Noir; and Cabernet Franc. Other *Vitis vinifera* wines include semi-dry Cascade Riesling, oak-aged Fireside Chardonnay, and Luna Rossa Reserve, a Lemberger / Pinot Noir blend. Cascata's other blends include Red Bouquet, a blend of Baco Noir, Leon Millot, and Maréchal Foch; Odds and Ends, a semi-dry

Castel Grisch Estate Winery

red blend; Lambrusco-style, semi-sweet Awakening Rosé; and Regatta Red.

Cascata Winery also produces Morning Blush, made from Cayuga White grapes; Sweet Iris, a semi-sweet wine made from Delaware; and semi-sweet Celebration Iris, also made from Delaware. The Winery's speciality wines include Cranberry Bog Mead, Elderberry Dessert Wine, Pear Wine, and Blushing Flamingo Spumante.

18. *Castel Grisch Estate Winery*
Castel Grisch Estate Winery, 3380 County Route 28, Watkins Glen, NY 14891, www.fingerlakes-ny.com/castelgrisch, (607) 535-9614, is located several miles north of Watkins Glen, off County Route 23. The estate was founded by a Swiss family. Barb and Tom Malina own and manage the Manor, Bavarian deli, and Winery, which produces oak-aged Chardonnay; Alsace-style Gewürztraminer; Johannisberg Riesling; Cabernet Franc; and semi-dry Chablis Grand Cru, a Chardonnay / Riesling blend; Cayuga White; Vidal Blanc; and Baco Noir.

The Winery's blends include Seneca Dream White, a Niagara / Delaware blend; semi-dry Seneca Blush, a blend of Chardonnay, Riesling, and Baco Noir; Seneca Dream Red, a Catawba / Vincent blend; and Estate Reserve Burgundy, a blend of Cabernet Franc, Chancellor, and Chardonnay.

The Winery also produces Chardonnay Ice Wine and Vidal and Riesling Ice Wine, dessert wines made in the traditional German "Eiswein" style. In addition to the indoor dining area, dining on the deck provides a sweeping view of Seneca Lake.

Seneca Lake Vineyards

CHAPTER 6

Seneca Lake Wineries—East Side

"By insisting on having your bottle pointing to the north when the cork is being drawn, and calling the waiter Max, you may induce an impression on your guests which hours of labored boasting might be powerless to achieve. For this purpose, however, the guests must be chosen as carefully as the wine."

Saki, *The Chaplet*

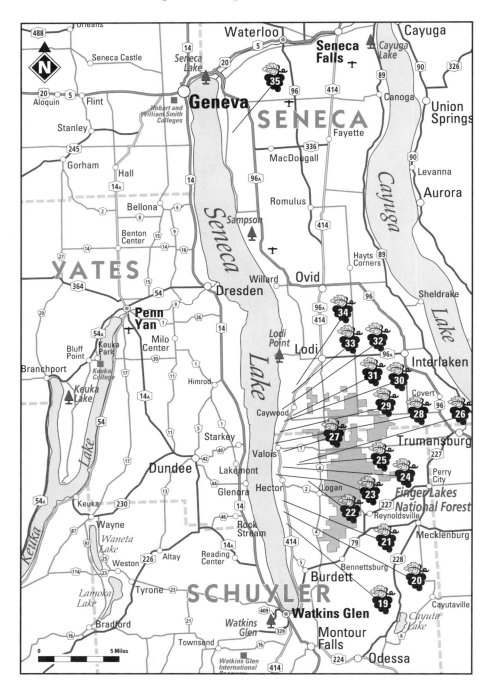

CHAPTER 6

Seneca Lake Wineries—East Side

19. Atwater Estate Vineyards

Atwater Estate Vineyards, 5055 Route 414, Hector, NY 14841, (607) 546-8463, www.atwatervineyards.com, is owned by Ted Marks and managed by his daughter Ann and son-in-law Phil Hazlitt, who is also the winemaker. The winery is located eight miles north of Watkins Glen. Atwater Estate Vineyards produces Dry Riesling, Semi-dry Riesling, Alsatian-style Gewürztraminer, Pinot Noir, and Chardonnay, made from grapes from over 20-year-old grapevines and fermented in French oak.

The winery's blends include Estate White, a Chardonnay / Seyval Blanc blend; Estate Red, a blend of Maréchal Foch, Chelois, and Chancellor; medium-bodied Reserve Red, a blend of Maréchal Foch, Chelois, and Cabernet Franc; and Bordeaux-style Meritage, a blend of Cabernet Sauvignon, Cabernet Franc, and Merlot, fermented and aged in French oak. Atwater Estates also produces two dessert wines: Late Harvest Vignoles and Vidal Ice Wine, made from grapes picked and pressed after they have frozen on the vine.

In addition, Atwater Estates Vineyards makes the Somerset series of wines with labels that capture the essence of traditional English gardens. The Atwater family resided in Somerset County, England, prior to settling in America in 1637. Somerset series blends include Somerset White, a Diamond / Cayuga White blend; Somerset Blush, a Catawba / Cayuga White blend; and semi-dry Somerset Red, fermented in stainless steel.

20. Chateau LaFayette Reneau Winery

Chateau LaFayette Reneau Winery, 5081 Route 414, Hector, NY 14841, (607) 546-2062, www.clrwine.com, was established in 1985 by Dick and Betty Reno.

Chateau LaFayette Reneau produces barrel-fermented Chardonnay; barrel-fermented and -aged Proprietor's Reserve Chardonnay, made from select grapes; Dry Riesling; Johannisberg Riesling; Pinot Noir Blanc; oak-aged Cabernet

Sauvignon; Cabernet Sauvignon Owner's Reserve; Pinot Noir; and oak-aged Merlot.

Chateau LaFayette Reneau's blends include Cuvée Rouge, a blend of *Vitis vinifera* and hybrid grapes; Seyval-Chardonnay; Meadow Mist, a Catawba / Baco Noir blend; and Niagara Mist. The Winery also produces Blanc de Blancs sparkling wine made from Chardonnay grapes fermented in *Méthode Champenoise*-style. Chateau LaFayette Reneau has a large deck that provides a beautiful view of Seneca Lake.

21. Bloomer Creek Vineyard

Bloomer Creek Vineyard, 5315 Route 414, Hector, NY 14841, (607) 546-5000, is owned by Kim Engle, Debra Bermingham, and Scott Signori. The winery produces oak-aged Chardonnay that is aged sur lies, off-dry Riesling, Cabernet Franc, Gamay Noir from estate-grown grapes, and Cayuga White with a touch of sweetness.

The winery also makes semi-sweet Heritage Raspberry fruit wine and Red Emperor, a blend of Cabernet Franc and French-American hybrid varieties. Bloomer Creek's Stonecat Café offers a variety of food to accompany their wine.

22. Red Newt Cellars

Red Newt Cellars, 3675 Tichenor Road, Hector, NY 14841, (607) 546-4100, www.rednewt.com, is named for the Eastern Spotted Red Newt, which the owners view as one of nature's most beautiful but often overlooked creatures. The winery is owned and managed by Debra and David Whiting, who is the winemaker. 1998 was the first vintage at Red Newt Cellars.

The winery produces barrel-fermented Chardonnay, aged sur lies; Reserve Riesling; Gewürztraminer; Cabernet Sauvignon; Cabernet Franc; Pinot Noir; and Merlot. Its blends include semi-dry Red Newt White, a Vidal Blanc / Cayuga White blend; Red Eft, a blend of Cabernet Franc, Merlot, Cabernet Sauvignon, Pinot Noir, and Syrah; and Syrah-Cabernet Franc. Howard Goldberg of the New York

Times refers to "David B. Whiting's pointedly food oriented wines ... lean, clean, brisk, precisely and intensely flavored, elegant." Mort Hochstein of *Wine Enthusiast* magazine adds that Mr. Whiting "raised the quality bar" in the Finger Lakes Region.

The Red Newt Cellars winetasting bar is located in a 2,100-square-foot room also used as a banquet facility with a capacity of several hundred people. Red Newt's "Bistro," an upscale restaurant managed by Debra Whiting, seats 50 but can accommodate 250 for catered events. Bistro offers an innovative and ever-changing menu. Seating is available in the dining room or outdoors on a covered deck that provides a sweeping view of the Seneca Lake Valley.

23. Leidenfrost Vineyards
Leidenfrost Vineyards, 5677 Route 414, Hector, NY 14841, (607) 546-2800, is owned by John Leidenfrost, who is also the winemaker. The winery is located on a farm that has been in the Leidenfrost family since 1947. Leidenfrost Vineyards produces Chardonnay, Riesling, Semi-dry Riesling, Gewürztraminer, Semi-dry Gewürztraminer, Pinot Noir, Pinot Noir Reserve, Merlot, Cabernet Franc, and Cabernet Sauvignon, which is blended with small quantities of Cabernet Franc and Merlot. Leidenfrost's wines made from French-American grapes are Cayuga White and Baco Noir.

The winery's blends include non-vintage Baco Beaujolais, a Pinot Noir / Baco Noir blend; semi-dry Log Cabin Red, a Cayuga White / Baco Noir blend; semi-sweet Log Cabin White; and semi-sweet Seneca Rosé, a blend of Cayuga White, Catawba, Merlot, and Gewürztraminer. Leidenfrost also makes semi-sweet Pink Catawba and Late Harvest Riesling dessert wine.

24. Hazlitt 1852 Vineyards
Hazlitt 1852 Vineyards, 5712 Route 414, Hector, NY, 14841, (607) 546-9463, www.hazlitt1852.com, is located on a farm

that has been in the family since 1852 and is currently managed by fifth and sixth generation Hazlitts. Jerry and Elaine Hazlitt, who had been vineyardists, opened the winery in 1985. Doug Hazlitt is the winery manager.

Hazlitt 1852 Vineyards produces oak-fermented Chardonnay, Riesling, Pinot Gris, Gewürztraminer, Cabernet Sauvignon, Merlot, and Cabernet Franc. Hazlitt blends include semi-dry Schooner White, a blend of Chardonnay, Riesling, and Cayuga White; semi-sweet White Stag, a blend of Cayuga White, Ravat (Vignoles), and Vidal Blanc; semi-sweet Cabin Fever, a Catawba / Cayuga White blush; and Schooner Red, a blend of Baco Noir, Cabernet Franc, Cabernet Sauvignon, and Merlot.

The winery also produces popular Red Cat, a Catawba / Baco Noir blend; Lame Duck, a sparkling wine made from native-American grapes; and specialty wines, such as semi-sweet Bramble Berry, made with Finger Lakes grapes and the essence of red and black raspberries; as well as Late Harvest Ravat 51 dessert wine from grapes picked in late October.

Hazlitt's tasting room, with a horseshoe-shaped tasting bar, has a friendly, relaxed atmosphere fostered by members of the Hazlitt family. The room is a compact museum of local history, with Seneca Indian artifacts, antique tools, and other local memorabilia.

25. *Logan Ridge Estates Winery*

Logan Ridge Estates Winery, 3800 Ball Diamond Road (off Route 414), Hector, NY 14841, www.loganridge.com, (607) 546-6600, is located 15 minutes north of Watkins Glen. The Winery is situated high on a hillside with a beautiful view of Seneca Lake. The winetasting room is located in what was the natatorium of the mansion in which one of the owners used to live.

Logan Ridge Estates produces five dry white wines: Reserve Chardonnay, fermented in French oak barrels; Chardonnay, fermented and aged in stainless steel; Pinot

Logan Ridge Estates Winery

Blanc, fermented in oak barrels; barrel-fermented Vidal Blanc; and Estate White, a blend of Cayuga White, Vignoles, and Vidal Blanc. The Winery's dry red wines include Pinot Noir, aged in French oak; Cabernet Franc; oak-aged Cabernet Sauvignon; oak-aged Merlot; and Cabernet, a blend of Cabernet Franc and Cabernet Sauvignon.

Logan Ridge Estates also produces semi-sweet wines: Rosé of Cabernet Franc; Riesling; Cayuga White; and Estate Blush, a blend of Cayuga White, Baco Noir, Lakemont, Reliant, and Vanessa. Estate Red is a Baco Noir / DeChaunac blend. In addition, the Winery makes light-bodied Rosé of Sangiovese with a touch of sweetness, Port with toasty oak flavor, and two sweet fruit wine blends of juice and white wine: Logan Berry and Black Cherry.

Logan Ridge Estates Winery has a award-winning restaurant, "Petioles." The beautiful main room can accommodate over 200 people for catered special events. Additional rooms are available for meetings and for intimate dining.

26. Tickle Hill Winery

Tickle Hill Winery, 3839 Ball Diamond Road (off Route 414), Hector, NY 14841, (607) 546-7740, is owned by Timothy and Valerie Rosbaugh. Their granddaughter, Brooke, named the Winery when she experienced a sensation in the pit of her stomach while traveling up and down the hill on which the Winery is located.

Tickle Hill produces light-bodied Pinot Noir, dry Cayuga White, dry Niagara, and hearty, dry Rosé. The Winery also makes semi-sweet wines: White Delight; Sweetie Pie; Muscat-like Tickle Phil; Tickle Me Pink Blush, made from Catawba grapes; Tickle My Fancy, made from Delaware grapes; and Susie Q, a Niagara / Delaware blend.

Tickle Hill Winery also produces Demi-sec Pink Champagne from Catawba and semi-dry Apple Apeel wine, a blend of several apple varieties, as well as two dessert wines: Peach Fuzz and Razzle Dazzle, made from raspberries.

27. Rasta Ranch Vineyards

Rasta Ranch Vineyards, 5882 Route 414, Hector, NY 14841, (607) 546-2974, www.anglefire.com/w13/rastaranch, is owned and managed by Diane Buglion-Mannion. The tasting room is housed in a circa 1860s barn near the vineyards and gardens in which aromatic herbs, perennial flowers, and bedding plants are grown.

Rasta Ranch Vineyards produces wine from native-American grapes, including Catawba Dry and dry Seneca Rain from Catawba grapes, and semi-dry Purple Haze and sweet Uncle Homer's Red from Concord grapes. The winery also produces wine from French-American hybrid grapes, such as Cayuga White, Seyval Blanc, Baco Noir, and dry Grateful Red and Sweet Forgiveness from Chelois.

The winery's blends include Whiter Shade of Pale, a Seyval Blanc / Cayuga White blend; and Piece of My Heart, a Concord / Catawba blend. Rasta Ranch also makes specialty wines: Sangria-style JaMa'ca Me Blush, made from Baco Noir; and semi-dry Arlo's Apple, a crisp, light wine made from New York State apples.

28. Finger Lakes Champagne House

Finger Lakes Champagne House, 6075 Route 414, Hector, NY 14841, (607) 546-5115, www.swedishhill.com, is located 12 miles north of Watkins Glen. The Champagne House features champagnes of Swedish Hill Winery and Goose Watch Winery. Swedish Hill Winery champagnes include Naturel Champagne, a Chardonnay / Pinot Noir blend; Brut Champagne, bottle-fermented in the *méthode champenoise* from Chardonnay and Pinot Noir grapes; and semi-dry Blanc de Blancs. Swedish Hill also makes semi-dry Riesling Cuvée Reserve and semi-sweet Spumante Blush.

Goose Watch Winery's Champagnes include Pinot Noir Brut Rosé and dry Blanc de Noir. Goose Watch also produces semi-sweet Golden Spumante and semi-sweet Sparkling Pear, made from New York State Bartlett pears.

29. Standing Stone Vineyard

Standing Stone Vineyard, 9934 Route 414, Hector, NY 14841, (800) 803-7135, www.standingstonewines.com, is owned and managed by Tom and Marti Macinski. The winery was named for the People of the Standing Stone for whom the early Dutch fur traders in the region searched. Standing Stone Vineyard produces Chardonnay, oak-aged Smokehouse Chardonnay, Reserve Chardonnay, Dry and Semi-dry Riesling, and Alsatian-style Gewürztraminer. Standing Stone's Dry Vidal Blanc is aged in oak barrels; the winery also makes a popular Semi-dry Vidal Blanc wine.

Standing Stone Vineyard was one of the earliest vineyards in the region to grow Cabernet Franc grapes, from which it produces an award-winning wine. The winery also produces Merlot, Pinot Noir, and Reserve Cabernet Sauvignon. Its blends include Smokehouse White, a Vidal Blanc / Pinot Gris blend; and Pinnacle, a blend of Cabernet Sauvignon, Cabernet Franc, and Merlot.

Standing Stone Vineyard owns the original Gold Seal *Vitis vinifera* vineyards on Seneca Lake. The winery has a popular deli that offers food to accompany their fine wines.

30. Bagley's Poplar Ridge Vineyards

Bagley's Poplar Ridge Vineyards, 9782 Route 414, Valois, NY 14841, (607) 582-6421, is owned by David Bagley, whose motto, as has been displayed on his wine labels, is "wine without bull." His goal is "to produce wines that people can enjoy and feel comfortable with on any occasion. We hate to see people intimidated by the pretentious attitudes ... that take all the fun out of wine."

Bagley's Poplar Ridge Vineyards produces Chardonnay, Riesling, and Riesling Reserve, as well as wine from French-American hybrid grapes, such as Cayuga White. Cayuga Reserve is a blend of Cayuga White, Ravat (Vignoles), Vidal Blanc, Baco Noir, and Chelois.

The winery's blends include Landlocked White and

Valois Rouge, a Carmine / Seyval Blanc blend. The winery also produces Bagley's Brut sparkling wine and a premium apple wine, One-Eyed Jack. Poplar Ridge Vineyards has planted additional Cabernet Sauvignon, Cabernet Franc, Merlot, Malbec, and Traminette vines in recent years.

31. Shalestone Vineyards

Shalestone Vineyards, 9681 Route 414, Lodi, NY 14860, (607) 582-6600, www.shalestonevineyards.com, specializes in dry red wines. The owners and managers are Kate and Rob Thomas, who is also the winemaker. In 2002, Shalestone added a 2,500-square-foot production facility, built into the ground to take advantage of stable ambient temperatures.

Rob Thomas has developed wine with depth, personality, and complexity from red *Vitis vinifera* grapes grown in his Seneca Lake vineyards. A passion for drinking and producing red wine led to the Shalestone slogan: RED IS ALL WE DO.

The winery produces wine for those who can appreciate the importance of wine in life and want to experience the essence of wine from the Finger Lakes Region. Merlot, Cabernet Sauvignon, Cabernet Franc, and Pinot Noir grapes are used to produce varietal wines. The winery also makes red blends, such as Red Legend, a blend of Cabernet Franc, Leon Millot, and Merlot.

32. Silver Thread Vineyards

Silver Thread Vineyards, 1401 Caywood Road (off Route 414), Lodi, NY 14860, www.silverthreadwine.com, (607) 582-6116, is an environmentally sensitive winery that produces wine from organic grapes. The winery began producing wine in 1991 from 10-year-old vineyards. In the late 1980s, Silver Thread Vineyards "began to practice organic sustainable farming by eliminating synthetic chemical pesticides and fertilizers and seeking to work in harmony with the natural ecosystem." Silver Thread wines are minimally processed in a low-tech traditional cellar built in 1995.

The winery is set into the hillside for natural temperature control, augmented by passive solar heat and a wood-burning stove. Water is gravity fed from a spring adjacent to the vineyard. The winery, like the vineyard, is designed to function within the natural system. Silver Thread Vineyards has vineyards at its Caywood site and on the east side of Keuka Lake.

The winery produces Chardonnay, fermented in American oak barrels; Chardonnay Reserve, fermented in French oak barrels; Dry Riesling; Gewürztraminer; and Pinot Noir, using partial wild-yeast fermentation and aged in American and French oak barrels. Silver Thread Vineyard's blends include Good Earth White, a blend of Cayuga White, Riesling, and Chardonnay; and Good Earth Rosé, a Pinot Noir / Gewürztraminer blend.

33. Wagner Vineyards

Wagner Vineyards, 9322 Route 414, Lodi, NY 14860, (607) 582-6450, www.wagnervineyards.com, established in 1979, is the only octagonal winery in the Finger Lakes Region. The efficient design has a center core used for fermenting and aging wine, surrounded by crushing and pressing facilities, fermenting tanks, bottling line, tasting room, and retail store. All Wagner wines are estate bottled, that is, they are made from grapes grown on the site of the winery.

The winery produces barrel-fermented Chardonnay and Chardonnay Reserve, medium-bodied Vintner's Chardonnay, medium-bodied Dry and Semi-dry Riesling, Dry and Semi-dry Gewürztraminer, full-bodied Cabernet Franc, oak-aged Cabernet Sauvignon, medium-bodied Merlot, oak-aged Reserve Pinot Noir, lightly oaked Grace House Pinot Noir, and semi-dry Pinot Noir Blush. Wagner's wine from French-American hybrid grapes includes semi-sweet Cayuga White, semi-dry Melody, barrel-fermented Seyval Blanc, oak-aged DeChaunac, and Vignoles.

Wagner Vineyards also produces blended wine, such as oak-aged Meritage, a Bordeaux-type blend; OCR (Octagon

Wagner Vineyards

Cellars Reserve) from red *Vitis vinifera* varieties; light-bodied, oak-aged Reserve Red; dry Reserve White; and semi-sweet Reserve Blush. The winery also produces semi-sweet Alta Blanc, Alta Blush, and red Alta B, which are named for Bill Wagner's mother. In addition, Wagner makes wine from native-American varieties, including Delaware and Niagara.

Wagner Vineyards uses the *méthode champenoise* to make Brut Champagne from Chardonnay and Pinot Noir grapes, as well as Riesling Champagne. The winery also makes dessert wines, such as Riesling Ice Wine, Vidal Ice Wine, Vignoles Ice Wine, and Late Harvest Vignoles. In 1983, Wagner opened the popular Ginny Lee Cafe, named for his granddaughter, at the winery to stress "the link between wine and food and the fact that wine is food."

In 1997, the Seneca Valley Brewing Company was added to Wagner Vineyards beginning with a 20-barrel, German-style brewhouse using three vessels: a mash mixer / kettle, a lauter tun, and a whirlpool. The microbrewery produces Captain Curry's ESB, a bitter, London-style, copper-colored ale; Dockside Amber Lager, a medium-bodied, malty Vienna-style lager; Grace House Honey Wheat, a light-bodied golden ale; Mill Street Pilsner, a pale straw-colored dry lager; and medium-bodied Seneca Trail Pale Ale. Seneca Valley Brewing Company also brews Caywood Station Stout, a robust, full-bodied oatmeal stout; and Sled Dog Doppelbock, a malty full-bodied lager.

The winery's deck and the Ginny Lee Café provide panoramic views of Seneca Lake. The winery, café, and microbrewery are handicapped-accessible.

34. *Lamoreaux Landing Wine Cellars*
Lamoreaux Landing Wine Cellars, 9224 Route 414, Lodi, NY 14680, (607) 582-6011, www.fingerlakes.net/lamoreaux, is owned and managed by Mark Wagner, whose family members have been vineyardists for decades. Lamoreaux Landing Wine Cellars, which is named for an old steamboat landing on

Lamoreaux Landing Wine Cellars

the property, was established in 1990.

The winery produces barrel-fermented Chardonnay, Dry Riesling, Semi-dry Riesling, Gewürztraminer, and four barrel-aged reds: Cabernet Sauvignon, Pinot Noir, Merlot, and Cabernet Franc. The winery's blends include Estate White, a blend of Chardonnay and Riesling, fermented in stainless steel; and Estate Red, a Pinot Noir / Cabernet Franc blend. Lamoreaux Landing also produces Blanc de Blancs from Chardonnay grapes and Brut, a Chardonnay / Pinot Noir blend sparking wine, both made by the *méthode champenoise*.

Lamoreaux Landing Wine Cellars was constructed in 1992, and an addition was built in 1996. The tall, narrow, multi-level winery with four large square columns in front catches visitors' eyes as they drive north along Route 414. It was designed by California architect Bruce Corson, son of Cornell President Emeritus Dale Corson.

35. *Nagy's New Land Vineyards and Winery*
Nagy's New Land Vineyards and Winery, 623 Lerch Road (off Route 96A), Geneva, NY 14456, www.nagyswines.com, (315) 585-4432, established in 1988, is owned and managed by Dale Nagy.

New Land Vineyards produces Chardonnay, aged in French oak; medium-bodied Dry Riesling, Semi-dry Riesling, Dry Gewürztraminer, Semi-dry Gewürztraminer, Pinot Noir Blanc, and lightly oaked Sauvignon Blanc, a little-grown variety in the Finger Lakes Region. The Winery also makes Cabernet Sauvignon; Pinot Noir, aged in American oak; and full-bodied Merlot. Its blends include Merlot / Cabernet; semi-sweet Nagy's White, aged in French oak; and semi-sweet Nagy's red, a Delaware / Pinot Noir blend.

New Land also makes specialty wines, such as Late harvest Riesling with 4% residual sugar and Late Harvest Sauvignon Blanc with 6% residual sugar.

Seneca Lake Wine Trail

The Seneca Lake Wine Trail is comprised of 24 Seneca Lake wineries that have combined to promote area winemaking and to join together in a number of special events each year. Also, many of the wineries conduct their own individual events throughout the year. The Seneca Lake Winery Association is located at 100 N. Franklin Street, Watkins Glen, NY 14891, www.senecalakewine.com, (877) 536-2717. Barbara Adams is the executive director.

Members of the Seneca Lake Wine Trail are:
- Amberg Wine Cellars
- Anthony Road Wine Co.
- Arcadian Estate Vineyards
- Atwater Estate Vineyards
- Cascata Winery at the Professors' Inn
- Castel Grisch Estate Winery
- Chateau LaFayette Reneau Winery
- Earle Estates Winery & Meadery
- Finger Lakes Champagne House
- Fox Run Vineyards
- Fulkerson Winery
- Glenora Wine Cellars
- Hazlitt 1852 Vineyards
- Lakewood Vineyards Winery
- Lamoreaux Landing Wine Cellars
- Logan Ridge Estates Winery
- Leidenfrost Vineyards
- Miles Wine Cellars
- Nagy's New Land Vineyards and Winery
- Prejean Winery
- Red Newt Cellars
- Seneca Shore Wine Cellars
- Torrey Ridge Winery
- Wagner Vineyards

NYStateWine.com / Chateau D'Esperant

The tasting room and gallery of NYStateWine.com is located at 29 North Franklin Street, Watkins Glen, NY 14891, (607) 535-2944. The tasting room, with a 27-foot, copper-topped tasting bar, showcases over 100 wines from 50 New York State wineries, including over two dozen Finger Lakes wineries. The gallery offers many wine-related gifts.

CHAPTER 7

Cayuga Lake Wineries — West Side

"Go thy way, eat thy bread with joy, and drink thy wine with a merry heart."

Bible, Ecclesiastes IX, 7

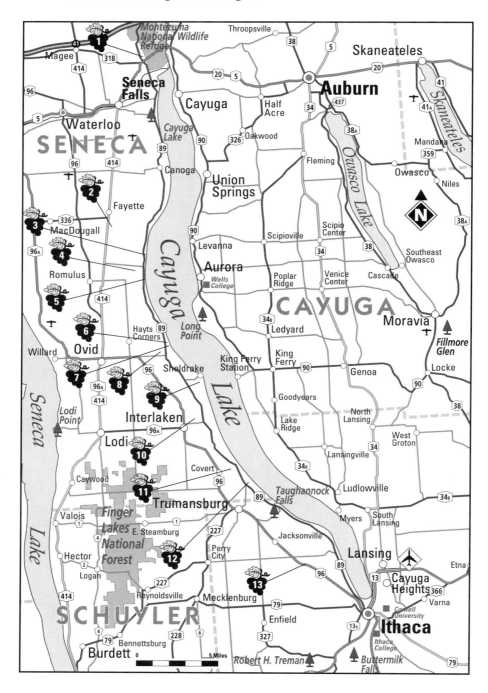

CHAPTER 7

Cayuga Lake Wineries—West Side

Swedish Hill Winery

1. Montezuma Winery

Montezuma Winery, 2981 Auburn Road (Corner of Routes 5 / 20 and 89), Seneca Falls, NY 13148, (315) 568-8190, is owned and managed by the Martin family, who also own Martin's Honey Farm & Meadery in Sterling, NY. The Winery produces dry Riesling, dry Vidal Blanc, dry Chancellor, semi-dry Seyval Blanc, semi-dry Cayuga White, and Canvasback Red, a light-bodied blend of DeChaunac and Cabernet Franc.

Montezuma also produces Dry, Semi-sweet, and Sweet Traditional Honey Wine (Mead). In addition, the Winery makes fruit wines, including Cherry Wine, Cranberry Bog, Pear Perfection, Just Peachy, Golden Delicious apple wine, Blue Moon blueberry wine, Strawberry Sunset wine, and Finale, an apricot dessert wine. Its blends include Lake Effect Blush, a cranberry / apple wine; and Johnny Apple Mead, a spiced honey / apple wine.

2. Swedish Hill Winery

Swedish Hill Winery, 4565 Route 414, Romulus, NY 14541, (315) 549-8326, www.swedishhill.com, located eight miles south of Seneca Falls, was founded in 1985. The Winery is owned and managed by Dick and Cindy Peterson. Dick manages the vineyard, and Cindy is the marketing manager.

Swedish Hill Winery produces Surfside Chardonnay; Reserve Chardonnay, barrel fermented with 100% malolactic fermentation; Dry Riesling; Semi-dry Riesling; and oak-aged Cabernet Franc. The Winery also produces semi-dry Vidal Blanc, semi-dry Cayuga White, semi-sweet Vignoles, and dry Maréchal Foch, as well as semi-sweet Delaware "Glenside Vineyards / Old Vines Reserve" and semi-sweet Country Concord.

Swedish Hill's blends include Viking White, a blend of Cayuga White, Melody, Chardonnay, Vignoles, and Vincent; oak-aged Viking Red, a blend of *Vitis vinifera* and French-American hybrid grapes; and oak-aged Optimus, a Bordeaux-style blend of Cabernet Sauvignon, Merlot, and Cabernet Franc.

The Svenska series of semi-sweet blended wines—White, Blush, and Red—is also popular. In addition, the Winery produces Naturel and Brut Champagne, Blanc de Blancs, Riesling Cuvée, and Spumante Blush. Its speciality wines include oak-aged Cynthia Marie Port; Glögg Wine, made with an extract imported from Sweden; Vignoles Late Harvest dessert wine; and Just Peachy and Radical Raspberry fruit wines.

Swedish Hill Winery has tours daily and offers horse-drawn wagon rides through the vineyards. The Winery has a deck and a picnic area and schedules many special events throughout the year. Swedish Hill Winery also has a retail store at 121 Cascade Road, Lake Placid, NY 12946, (518) 523-2498.

3. Lakeshore Winery

Lakeshore Winery, 5132 Route 89, Romulus, NY 14541, (315) 549-7075, www.lakeshorewinery.com, is owned and managed by John and Annie Bachman. Lakeshore Winery produces Chardonnay, Dry Riesling, Semi-dry Riesling, Cabernet Sauvignon, and Pinot Noir. The Winery also produces Cayuga White, Baco Noir, and Amarone, made from Baco Noir grapes. Its popular blends include Aunt Clara and Uncle Charlie, made principally from Catawba; Country Blush, mainly Catawba; Country Claret, a Baco Noir / Cayuga White blend; and Barbecue, principally Baco Noir.

Isaac Phillips Roberts, a founder of the College of Agriculture at Cornell University, was born in the house on Winery property on July 24, 1833, as noted by a New York State historical marker on Route 89 below the Winery.

Lakeshore Winery provides special activities for visitors, including Lakeshore Nouveau Weekend in early November to celebrate the harvest just completed. The Winery favors sit-down winetastings with food served between individual tastings to emphasize the fact that wine is food. Picnic facilities are available. The Lakeshore Winery winetasting room has a large stone fireplace that is used during the late fall, winter, and early spring. The Winery is accessible by boat; docking is available.

Knapp Winery

4. Knapp Winery

Knapp Winery, 2770 Ernsberger Road (County Road 128, off Route 89), Romulus, NY 14541, www.knappwine.com, (800) 869-9271, was established in 1972.

Knapp Winery is owned by the parent corporation of Glenora Wine Cellars and Logan Ridge Estates Winery. The principals are Gene Pierce, CEO of Glenora Wine Cellars, and Scott Welliver, president of Welliver-McGuire Construction. Ed Dalrymple was also one of the founders of the corporation.

Knapp Winery produces Barrel Reserve Chardonnay; Cayuga Lake Chardonnay, aged in stainless steel; Dry Riesling; Semi-dry Riesling; Pinot Noir with subtle oak; oak-aged Merlot; medium-bodied Cabernet Franc; oak-aged Cabernet Sauvignon; and Sangiovese. Knapp Winery also makes semi-sweet Vignoles, semi-dry Pasta White from Seyval Blanc, semi-dry Pasta Red from Baco Noir, and Kat Knapp from Catawba.

Knapp's blends include semi-sweet Dutchman's Breeches, a Vidal Blanc / Vignoles blend; semi-dry Lady's Slipper, a blend of Cabernet Sauvignon and Cayuga White; Pasta Rosé, a Seyval Blanc / Baco Noir blend; and light-bodied Prism, a classic Bordeaux blend. The Winery also produces Brandy, Ruby Port, Cherry and Peach Avinac cordials, Grappa, Strawberry Grappa, and Limoncello, a lemon-flavored Grappa.

Knapp's specialty wines include Vintner's Select Vignoles dessert wine and Mon Cherry and Jammin' Strawberry fruit wines. The Winery also makes Brut and semi-dry Blanc de Blancs sparkling wines. Knapp Winery is also known for its fine restaurant, which has emphasized fish and meat from the region and locally grown vegetables.

5. Goose Watch Winery

Goose Watch Winery, 5480 Route 89, Romulus, NY 14541, (315) 549-2599, www.goosewatch.com, is owned by Dick and Cindy Peterson, who also own Swedish Hill Winery. The wine-tasting room is in a beautifully restored century-old barn situated in Goose Watch Farm's chestnut grove. The farm includes an aquaculture trout operation.

Goose Watch Winery produces Pinot Gris; Pinot Gris Barrel Reserve, fermented in French oak with malolactic fermentation and sur lies aging; Viognier; barrel-aged Cabernet Sauvignon; Merlot; Cabernet Franc; and medium-bodied Lemberger. The Winery also produces semi-dry Melody; dry Traminette, a Gewürztraminer-type wine; and Villard Blanc, reminiscent of Sauvignon Blanc; Diamond; and Rosé of Isabella.

Goose Watch's blends include Renaissance Red and Bayside Blush, a Cayuga White / Pinot Noir blend. The Winery also makes Pinot Noir Brut Rosé Champagne, Finale White Port, and Golden Spumante sparkling wine. Goose Watch's specialty wines include Bartlett Pear fruit wine and Strawberry Splendor dessert wine.

Visitors to Goose Watch Winery are invited to bring a picnic lunch to enjoy on the deck or to snack on local cheese and other delicacies, including smoked trout, from Goose Watch Farm. The Winery offers horse-drawn wagon vineyard tours on weekend afternoons. Goose Watch Winery, which is located 15 minutes south of Seneca Falls, is accessible by boat. Docking is available.

6. Cayuga Ridge Estate Winery

Cayuga Ridge Estate Winery, 6800 Route 89, Ovid, NY (607) 869-5158, www.cayugaridge.com, is owned by Tom and Susie Challen. The Winery produces Chardonnay, aged in French oak barrels; semi-dry Riesling; Cayuga Cuvée, a *Vitis vinifera* blend; and Cabernet Franc. Cayuga Ridge Estate also produces Cayuga White, Chancellor, and Reserve Chancellor, aged in American oak. Chancellor is one of the most notable French-American hybrid red varieties and is widely grown in France.

The Winery's specialty wines include Cranberry Frost and Cranberry Essence, essence of cranberry combined with white wine. In recent years, Tom has planted additional Chardonnay, Riesling, Gewürztraminer, Cabernet Sauvignon, Cabernet Franc, and Chancellor vines.

Cayuga Ridge Estate Winery

Cayuga Ridge Estate Winery sponsors a vigneron (rent-a-grapevine) program. Participants in the program lease, tend, and harvest grapes from 10, 20, or 30 grapevines. Vignerons visit the vineyard about five times during the growing season and learn how to prune, tie, cluster-thin, and harvest their rented vines. At harvest time, they have a choice of taking the grapes, selling them, or paying the winery to make wine from them. Cayuga Ridge also sells juice to home winemakers.

Cayuga Ridge Estate Winery sponsors events throughout the year, including an early October event for visitors to experience the picking and crushing / pressing of the harvested grapes. Picnic tables are available at the winery. The winery has a second winetasting bar in the loft; buses are welcome.

7. Thirsty Owl Wine Company

Thirsty Owl Wine Company, 6799 Elm Beach Road (off Route 89), Ovid, NY 14521, (866) 869-5805, www.thirstyowl.com, is owned by Ted Cupp. The origin of the winery's name is described on the back label of its bottles: "Years ago, a gentleman was stumbling home after a fine night of faster horses, younger women, and older wine, when he came across a 4 foot, 6 inch owl in his path. The owl stated: 'I have a deal for you. I won't interfere with your faster horses or younger women if you share your older wine with me. In return, I will keep the birds and critters out of your vineyard.' Thus the deal was made. The owl guards the vineyard, and the gentleman shares with his thirsty friend the finest wines in New York."

Thirst Owl Wine Company, which opened in 2002, produces lightly oaked Chardonnay, semi-sweet Riesling, medium-oaked Merlot, and light, crisp Vidal Blanc. The winery's blends include Cabernet Rosé, a Cabernet Franc / Cayuga White blend; and Red Moon, a blend of Cabernet Franc, DeChaunac, and Baco Noir.

Thirsty Owl plans a bistro, a walkway along its 2,200-foot lakefront, and a dock to allow visitors to come by boat.

8. Hosmer Winery

Hosmer Winery, 6999 Route 89, Ovid, NY 14521, (607) 869-3393, is owned and managed by Cameron and Maren Hosmer. The Winery produces oak-aged Chardonnay, barrel-fermented Limited Release Chardonnay, Dry Riesling, semi-sweet Riesling, Pinot Gris, oak-aged Pinot Noir, medium-bodied Cabernet Franc, as well as semi-dry Cayuga White and off-dry Seyval Blanc.

Hosmer's blends include Alpine, a Chardonnay / Seyval Blanc blend with a hint of oak; semi-sweet Carousel Blush, a Cayuga White / Catawba blend; oak-aged House Red, a Cabernet Franc / DeChaunac blend; and semi-sweet Fireside Red. The Winery also makes semi-sweet Raspberry Rhapsody, white wine infused with local raspberries; sweet Raspberry Royale, a fortified dessert wine with local raspberries added; and semi-sweet Sangria. The Winery's speciality wines include sweet Late Harvest Riesling and brut Sparkling Wine, made from Cayuga White grapes fermented using the *Méthode Champenoise*.

Hosmer Winery has a spacious winetasting facility located near the vineyards, as well as a gift shop. Light food items are sold, and picnic tables are available.

9. Sheldrake Point Vineyards

Sheldrake Point Vineyards, 7448 County Road 153 (off Route 89), Ovid, NY 14521, www.sheldrakepoint.com, (607) 532-9401, is located in a renovated 1850 farmstead. Sheldrake Point's first vintage, using purchased grapes, was 1997. The 1999 vintage was the first from their vineyards.

The winery produces barrel-fermented and -aged Waterfall Chardonnay, Barrel Reserve Chardonnay, Dry Riesling, semi-dry Sheldrake Spring Riesling, Pinot Gris, oak-aged Cabernet Franc, oak-aged Pinot Noir, Merlot, and Gamay. Sheldrake Point's blends include Petite Dry Rosé, a blend of six varieties; Summer Blush; Luckystone Red, a Rougeon / Baco Noir blend; and Barrel Reserve Merganser Meritage, a Bordeaux-style blend of Merlot, Cabernet Sauvignon, and Cabernet Franc. The winery also produces Raspberry Splash, a blend of wine and fresh New York State raspberries.

Sheldrake Point Vineyards has a café that offers creative appetizers, tapas, sandwiches, light fare, and seasonal entrées prepared to complement their wine. The café's food may be enjoyed on the deck overlooking Cayuga Lake or at picnic tables around the farm and on the beach.

10. Lucas Vineyards

Lucas Vineyards, 3862 County Road 150 (off Route 89), Interlaken, NY 14847, www.lucasvineyards.com, (607) 532-4825, is located 18 miles north of Ithaca. The winery, the oldest on Cayuga Lake, is owned and managed by Ruth Lucas. Bill Lucas spent many years as a tugboat captain on the waters of the eastern seaboard, which explains the origin of the names of Tugboat Red and Tugboat White wines.

Lucas Vineyards produces Chardonnay, Dry Riesling, Semi-dry Riesling, Gewürztraminer, Cabernet Franc, Seyval Blanc, semi-dry Cayuga White, and semi-sweet Vignoles. The winery's blends include Stars, a Chardonnay / Cayuga White blend; Blues, a Seyval Blanc / Cayuga White blend; oak-aged, semi-dry Harbor Moon , a Vidal Blanc / Cayuga White blend; semi-dry Captain's Belle, a French-American hybrid blend named for Ruth Lucas; Tugboat White, a blend of Cayuga White, Vidal Blanc, and Vignoles; semi-sweet Butterfly; Dry Dock, made from oak-aged Baco Noir; and the popular semi-dry Tug Boat Red.

Lucas Vineyards also produces Late Harvest Riesling dessert wine and Blanc de Blancs Champagne, made from Chardonnay grapes using the *Méthode Champenoise*. The winery has an extensive gift shop, and picnic facilities are available. Lucas Vineyards produces personalized wine labels for any occasion.

Lucas Vineyards

11. Americana Vineyards Winery

Americana Vineyards Winery, 4367 East Covert Road, Interlaken, NY 14847, www.americanavineyards.com, (607) 387-6801, is located off Route 89, 14 miles north of Ithaca. The Winery is owned and managed by Joe Gober. Americana Winery, the second-oldest winery on Cayuga Lake, has been making wine since the early 1980s.

Americana Vineyards Winery produces Chardonnay, fermented and aged in European oak; Dry Riesling; Cabernet Franc, aged in French oak; semi-dry Cayuga White; and full-bodied Baco Noir. Americana's blends include Finger Lakes Chablis, a Chardonnay / Cayuga blend; Americana Blush, a blend of Delaware, Baco Noir, and Vincent; semi-dry Revolutionary Red, a blend of Baco Noir, Vincent, Maréchal Foch, and DeChaunac; semi-sweet Indian Summer, a Baco Noir / Catawba blend, reminiscent of an Italian Lambrusco; and November Harvest, a Sangria-like blend of Concord, Cayuga White, and Catawba.

The Winery also produces Americana White from Catawba grapes, Crystal Lake from Niagara grapes, and Sweet Rosie dessert wine from Ives grapes. Americana Vineyards Winery has a large outdoor pavilion for picnicking and outdoor wine-tastings.

12. Frontenac Point Vineyard

Frontenac Point Vineyard, 9501 Route 89, Trumansburg, NY 14886, (607) 387-9619, www.frontenacpoint.com, is located 12 miles north of Ithaca. Jim and Carol Doolittle planted their vineyard in 1978 and opened their winery in 1982.

In 1975, Jim earned a degree in viticulture from Cornell University and, as an employee of the New York State Department of Agriculture, helped to draft the Farm Winery Bill of 1976. Carol, previously editor of the *American Wine Society Journal*, organized the first New York State Fair commercial wine competition. Frontenac Point Vineyard makes wine from European and French-American hybrid grapes.

Frontenac Point produces oak-aged Chardonnay; dry Riesling; Pinot Noir; Vidal Blanc; Frontenac White, made from Seyval Blanc grapes; full-bodied Chambourcin; Chameleon, made with Pinot Noir grapes; and semi-dry Clos Frontenac Rosé, made with Chambourcin grapes.

Frontenac Point Vineyard also produces blends, such as dry Medley, a blend of Chardonnay, Vidal Blanc, and Seyval Blanc; oak-aged Proprietor's Reserve White, a blend of Chardonnay and Vidal Blanc; and oak-aged Proprietor's Reserve Red, a Pinot Noir / Chelois blend. Frontenac Point's speciality wines include brut Méthode Champenoise, a sparkling blanc de noir; Blanc de Noir, made from Pinot Noir grapes; Port Blanc, a late Harvest Ravat (Vignoles) dessert wine; and Port Frontenac dessert wine.

13. Bellwether Hard Cider Company
Bellwether Hard Cider Company, 1609 Trumansburg Road, Ithaca, NY 14850, (607) 272-4337, www.cidery.com, is located off Route 96, south of Trumansburg. Bellwether Hard Cider Company, owned by Bill and Cheryl Barton, produces "Original" Hard Cider; The Perry, fermented from Bartlett and Bosc pears; Apple-Peach Hard Cider; bottle-conditioned Hard Cider, made with Northern Spy apples; and Bittersweet Cider.

The Bartons have made test batches of cider from "old-fashioned" apple varieties with names like Brown Snout, Chisel Jersey, Ellis bitter, Fox Whelp, Hereford Redstreak, Kingston Black, Michelin, Somerset Redstreak, Tremlett's Bitter, and Brown Thorn. They are working with Cornell University to evaluate European varieties of cider apples, especially those with bittersweet characteristics. Adding these varieties to cider increases acid and tannin.

CHAPTER 8

Cayuga Lake Wineries—East Side

"Drink no longer water, but use a little wine for thy stomach's sake and thy often infirmities."

Bible, I Timothy 5:23

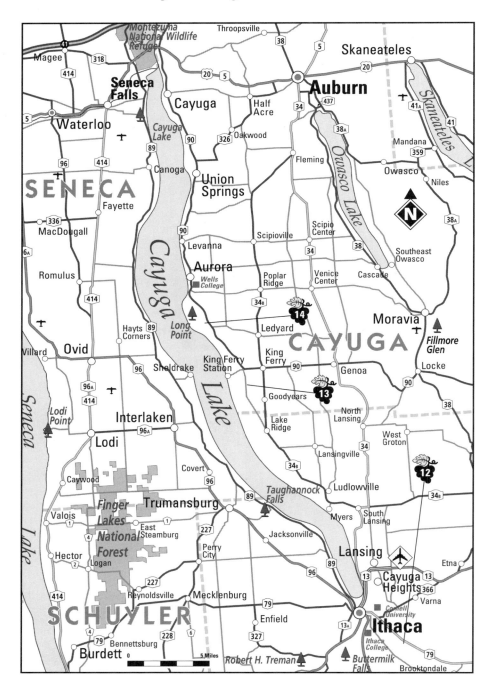

CHAPTER 8

Cayuga Lake Wineries—East Side

12. *Six Mile Creek Vineyard*

Six Mile Creek Vineyard, 1551 Slaterville Road (Route 79), Ithaca, NY 14850, (607) 272-9463, www.sixmilecreek.com, is owned and managed by Nancy Battistella. The winery is located in a restored turn-of-the-century Dutch Reform barn of post and beam construction.

Six Mile Creek Vineyard produces Chardonnay and Chardonnay Reserve, aged in French oak; dry Riesling; Pinot Noir; Merlot; full-bodied Quintessence, made from lightly oak-aged Cabernet Sauvignon; Cabernet Franc; and Ravat Vignoles.

Six Mile Creek Vineyard blends include Ithaca White, a blend of Cayuga White, Riesling, and Chardonnay; semi-dry Pasa Tiempo, a Riesling / Seyval Blanc blend; Cascadilla White, a blend of Seyval Blanc, Vidal Blanc, and Traminette; semi-dry Odyssey, a blend of Traminette, Chambourcin, and Leon Millot; Ithaca Red, a Maréchal Foch-based blend, aged in American oak; and semi-sweet Dolce Vita, a Maréchal Foch / Chambourcin blend.

The winery has a gift shop, picnic facilities, and a banquet room. The property overlooks picturesque Six Mile Creek.

13. *King Ferry Winery*

King Ferry Winery, 658 Lake Road (off Route 34B), King Ferry, NY 13081, (315) 364-5100, www.treleavenwines.com, is owned and managed by Peter and Tacie Saltonstall. Peter is the winemaker, and Tacie is the marketing manager. King Ferry Winery labels their wine "Treleaven" because the Saltonstalls bought the property for their vineyards and Winery from the Treleaven family. Picnic facilities are available at the Winery.

The Winery produces Merlot, Pinot Noir, oak-aged Main Chardonnay, oak-aged Reserve Chardonnay, stainless-steel-aged Silver Lining Chardonnay, Dry Riesling, Semi-dry Riesling, and Gewürztraminer. King Ferry blends include Reserve Melange, a Merlot / Cabernet Franc blend; Melange, a Merlot / Cabernet Franc blend with a touch of sweetness; and semi-dry Saumon, a Merlot / Vidal Blanc blend. The Winery also produces Spätgold, a heavily botrytised Riesling desert wine; and Apple Mystique, a sweet apple wine made with Liberty and Northern Spy apples grown in New York State.

Peter Saltonstall blends his Chardonnays to obtain the creamy, complex, and rich flavor of Chardonnays made in Meursault, France, in southern Burgundy. Peter ferments about 75 percent of his Chardonnay in French Vosges oak barrels; the oak imparts a slight creaminess and a touch of smokiness to the wine. The barrels hold about 60 gallons, which is the ideal size because of the ratio of the inside surface area of the barrel to the volume of wine. Treleaven Rieslings retain the delicate character of the fruit through months of temperature-controlled fermentation.

14. Long Point Winery

Long Point Winery, 1485 Lake Road (off Route 90), Aurora, NY 13026, (315) 364-6990, www.longpointwinery.com, was established in 1999. It is owned and managed by Gary and Rosemary Barletta.

Long Point Winery produces barrel-fermented Chardonnay; barrel-select Chardonnay Reserve, aged in French and Hungarian oak; dry Sauvignon Blanc; Cabernet Sauvignon; Merlot with a cedar oak frame; Merlot Reserve, framed in oak; Syrah also with an oak frame; Zinfandel; barrel-select Zinfandel Reserve, aged in French and Hungarian oak; and Vidal Blanc.

Long Point Winery's blends include semi-dry Ciera Rosé, a Vidal Blanc / Grenache blend; light-bodied Cambrie, a Beaujolais-like blend based on Grenache; and sweet Moon Puppy, a lightly oaked blend that is primarily Cabernet Franc.

Cayuga Wine Trail

The Cayuga Wine Trail, organized in 1982, was the first wine trail in the Finger Lakes Region and, in fact, in New York State. 13 wineries currently participate as members of the Cayuga Wine Trail:

- Americana Vineyards Winery
- Bellwether Hard Cider Co.
- Cayuga Ridge Estate Winery
- Goose Watch Winery
- Hosmer Winery
- King Ferry Winery
- Knapp Winery
- Lakeshore Winery
- Long Point Winery
- Lucas Vineyards
- Sheldrake Point Vineyards
- Six Mile Creek Vineyard
- Swedish Hill Winery

All of the wineries are on the west side of Cayuga Lake except for King Ferry Winery and Long Point Winery on the east side and Six Mile Creek Vineyard, which is southeast of the lake. Each winery sponsors its own special events during the growing season, and Wine Trail wineries work together on combined activities. The Cayuga Wine Trail website is: www.cayugawinetrail.com

CHAPTER 9

Winemaking Pioneers of the Region

"Wine is the most healthful and most hygienic of beverages."

Louis Pasteur, *Études Sur Le Vin*, Part I, Chapter 2

"A liter of wine contains one-eighth of our nutritional requirement and nine-tenths of good humor."

Professor Langouzy

Paul Garrett

Captain Paul Garrett, dean of American winemakers in the 1930s, became a multi-millionaire making and selling wine. The title of "captain" was not of military origin but was what his employees called him when they did not call him "the boss." He was born in North Carolina in 1863 and by the age of 14 was working for Medoc Vineyard, North Carolina's first commercial winery. It was owned by his father, country doctor Francis Garrett, and his uncle, Charles Garrett, who ran the winery.

Paul Garrett promoted wine made from the southern Scuppernong grape. He was the father of the Virginia Dare label, the best-selling wine in the United States in the 20 years prior to Prohibition. The original Virginia Dare wine was a blend of Concord, Scuppernong (which hid the foxy or grapey taste of the Concord grape), and California wine. He chose the name Virginia Dare—the first child born of English parents in America—because Scuppernong was the first American wine.

Paul Garrett established his first winery, Garrett & Company, in North Carolina in 1900, and by 1903 he owned five wineries in that state. He expanded into other states, and by 1913 he owned vineyards and wineries in Canandaigua, Hammondsport, and Penn Yan, as well as Mission Vineyard and Winery at Cucamonga, California. In 1919, he owned 17 plants processing grape juice or wine with a capacity of 10 million gallons in the states of California, Missouri, New York, North Carolina, Ohio, and Virginia.

Garrett could have retired as a multi-millionaire, but he held on to his wine empire, not believing that Prohibition would last. He lost millions of dollars on de-alcoholized wine, a cola-flavored grape drink, flavoring extracts, and grape concentrates. However, when Prohibition was repealed in 1933, he was the only vintner capable of marketing wine in every wet state. Also, he was the first winery executive to promote wine made from blending New York State and California juices.

Garrett attempted to convince California winegrowers of the advantage of blending the native-American *Vitis labrusca* grape varieties (high acid, low sugar) from the East, such as Concord, Delaware, and Ives, with the European *Vitis vinifera* grape varieties (low acid, high sugar) from the West. He was ahead of his time with this concept. By 1970, the large California wineries began to blend *Vitis labrusca* native-American concentrates and juice from other states with their juice.

One of Garrett's main themes was "American wine for Americans." He was in New York City promoting that concept when he contracted pneumonia and died on March 18, 1940, at the age of 76. He truly was a captain in his industry, and his idea of an American wine industry based on blends of East Coast and West Coast wines has survived. The Virginia Dare trademark was purchased and used by the Canandaigua Wine Company for a line of wines. By 1967, only white Virginia Dare had the Scuppernong taste.

Dr. Konstantin Frank

Dr. Konstantin Frank showed that *Vitis vinifera* grapes, the European varieties, could be grown in the Northeastern United States. Previous attempts at growing the less winter hardy European varieties in the Northeast had failed for over 200 years.

Other viticulturalists recommended French-American hybrid varieties for the region, a compromise on quality but a species of grapes more likely to survive severe winters. Dr. Frank, a strong-willed man, became controversial because of his public condemnation of French-American varieties. He asked why area vineyardists were not growing the world's premium varieties, such as Chardonnay and Riesling, and then he proved that they could be grown in the Finger Lakes Region.

Dr. Frank was born on July 4, 1899, in the Ukraine, the fourth of 10 children born to German parents. His father was a farmer and vineyardist. As a young man, Dr. Frank fought in the White Russian army. He studied agriculture at the Polytechnic Institute of Odessa and organized collective farms in southern Ukraine for the Communists. When he completed his studies, including enology and viticulture, he taught and conducted grape research at the local agricultural institute.

Dr. Frank liked to tell a story about an incident that occurred at the Institute of Viticulture and Enology in the Ukraine. He was responsible for the first three Ford tractors received in the Ukraine from the United States. He decided to determine how heavy a load the tractors could pull. Instead of lining the tractors up side by side, allowing each tractor to pull one third of the load, he aligned the tractors in tandem, with tractor two hitched front-to-back to tractor one, and tractor three between the load and tractor two. When all three tractors strained to pull the considerable load, structurally, they were not up to it. Tractor three, attached to the load, was literally pulled to pieces and destroyed. Some of the metal parts were stretched and some were broken. The tractor was not repairable; it had been demolished.

This incident occurred in the 1930s during the reign of Josef Stalin, and Dr. Frank was concerned about the repercussions of destroying one third of the Soviet Union's Ford tractors. He was not sure how far up the chain of command the information was passed but nothing happened, and no one ever reprimanded him.

During the German occupation in World War II, Dr. Frank was the director of the Institute of Viticulture and Enology in the Ukraine. When the war ended, he went to Austria and Bavaria to manage farm properties for the United States occupational forces.

Dr. Frank immigrated to the United States with his wife and three children in 1951, at 52 years of age. He did not speak English, and he had 40 dollars in his pocket. He washed dishes at an automat restaurant in New York City to earn the fare to the nearest grape research station, the New York State Agricultural Experiment Station at Geneva.

Dr. Frank described his background and told his supervisors that he hoped to use his experience. He said, "they let me hoe blueberries," and for two years he was given only menial chores. This experience provided him with some definite opinions of the Experiment Station at Geneva.

Dr. Frank watched Finger Lakes Region grapegrowers plant increasing acreage of French-American hybrid grapes. He asked why *Vitis vinifera* varieties were not being planted and was told that the winters were too cold and that the European varieties could not survive here. Dr. Frank had grown *Vitis vinifera* varieties in the Ukraine along the Dneiper River, "where the temperature goes to 40 below, where we had to bury the entire vine in winter, where when we spit, it froze before it hit the ground." He pointed out that *Vitis vinifera* vines did not die from the cold, but from disease, such as mildew and fungus, as well as from vine pests; furthermore, modern technology knew how to control these problems.

Charles Fournier, president of Gold Seal Winery, heard Dr. Frank's comments and realized that he might be right. Fournier had seen Chardonnay and Pinot Noir varieties survive at Epernay and Rheims, France, which are seven degrees of latitude farther north than Hammondsport. He had also seen temperatures drop below zero in the Champagne district of France. In 1953, Fournier hired Dr. Frank as a consultant to Gold Seal.

Dr. Frank convinced Fournier of the importance of winter hardy rootstock. He told Fournier that his research in the Ukraine had shown that, to survive the winter, *Vitis vinifera* vines should be grafted onto roots that would allow the ripening of the wood of the vine, the canes, before the first freeze of the winter. Dr. Frank and Fournier traveled around the Northeast in search of this type of rootstock, including trips to Ontario and Quebec.

They grafted *Vitis vinifera* vines, such as Cabernet Sauvignon, Chardonnay, Gewürztraminer, and Riesling, obtained from vineyards of the University of California at Davis, onto Canadian roots. Over a four-year period, thousands of grafted vines were planted. The winter of 1957 provided a severe test when the temperature dropped to 25 degrees below zero.

Gold Seal expanded their plantings of *Vitis vinifera* vines and had 70 acres planted by 1966. Dr. Frank bought property for a vineyard on Middle Road in Pulteney and planted his own vines. The first commercial New York State *Vitis vinifera* wines were introduced by Gold Seal in 1961; Dr. Frank called it "the second discovery of America."

By 1973, Dr. Frank's Vinifera Wine Cellars, Ltd., had expanded to 78 acres of vineyards and a winery capacity of 60,000 gallons. His Trockenbeerenauslese 1961 was served in the Executive Mansion in Albany and at the White House. Dr. Frank became a U.S. citizen and a vocal pro-American.

Dr. Frank built a winery behind his house and maintained a small pilot vineyard next to his home. In this vineyard, he planted at least two vines each of about 50 varieties / clones. Included were some little-known varieties, such as Fetjaska from Hungary, Kara Burni from Bulgaria, and Sereksiya Tschornay from the Ukraine. Dr. Frank died in 1985. The Frank tradition is being carried on and expanded upon by his son, Willy, and his grandson, Fred, whose previous position was managing director of Banfi Vineyards in Old Brookville, Long Island.

EPILOGUE

Showcasing the Finger Lakes Wine Region

by Fred Frank, President, Dr. Frank's Vinifera Wine Cellars

"Water separates the people of the world; wine unites them."

Anonymous

I am part of the third generation managing Dr. Frank's Vinifera Wine Cellars in Hammondsport. I have spent the last 20 years working in the wine business and have seen tremendous growth in the Finger Lakes Wine Region during that time. I have a degree in Business Administration from Cornell University and have studied winemaking at Geisenheim in Germany. I have tried through education and experience to obtain a well-rounded view of the world of wine from both a production and a marketing perspective.

The Finger Lakes appellation is the second largest in the U.S. behind only Napa Valley, as measured by the number of wineries. Few people realize this because no marketing group has been established specifically to promote Finger Lakes Region wines. Currently five wine trails in the Finger Lakes Region promote their own lake: the Canandaigua Wine Trail, the Keuka Lake Wine Trail, the Seneca Lake Wine Trail, the Cayuga Lake Wine Trail, and the Lake Ontario Wine Trail.

Although the individual wine trails work well in targeting visitors within a 100-mile radius of the lakes, their goal has not been promotion of the overall Finger Lakes Region. This goal is especially important in targeting visitors beyond the 100-mile radius of the lakes who have heard about the Finger Lakes Region but do not know the names of the individual lakes. The New York Wine & Grape Foundation does a great job promoting New York State wines; however, other organizations should be working in conjunction with the Wine & Grape Foundation in marketing Finger Lakes wines.

This shortsighted, provincial view is changing. We are members of two new Finger Lakes marketing organizations that should increase the visibility of our region in years to come. The Finger Lakes Wine Guild brings together a group of wineries focused on the production of food-oriented wines from classic European varieties. These are winegrowers dedicated to exploring how the region's sites, soils, and microclimates translate into the scents and flavors of world-class wines. The second group is the Finger Lakes Wine Alliance, which is inclusive of all wine styles found in the Finger Lakes Region. Member wineries work together to market Finger Lakes wines beyond the traditional 100-mile radius of the wine trails.

We are also part of two Finger Lakes tourism groups dedicated to promoting the region's attractions and natural beauty. The first group is Finger Lakes Wine Country that was created by Corning Enterprises, a division of Corning, Inc., which contracted several market research firms to determine a suitable scheme for local tourism promotion. The surveys indicated that the Finger Lakes Region wineries were the top-ranked regional tourist attraction. Corning Enterprises has joined with Steuben County, Schuyler County, Chemung County, the Corning Glass Museum, Wine Trails, and other attractions to raise a substantial marketing budget for promoting the region. The other organization, Finger Lakes Tourism has a larger membership of 12 counties and is also dedicated to promoting the Finger Lakes Region.

This cooperation among wineries, museums, restaurants, accommodations, and other attractions is unprecedented in the region. I am grateful to all four organizations for their leadership in getting us together as a team with the goal of greater awareness of the Finger Lakes Region, triggering increased tourism.

I am also grateful to Doug Knapp, founder of Knapp Winery, for sharing my vision of cooperation among the Finger Lakes Region wineries. Doug established the Finger Lakes Wine Festival in 1994, which has grown to showcase over 40 wineries each year. The festival is currently sponsored by Watkins Glen International at the famous Watkins Glen International Raceway. This event is an example of Finger Lakes wineries working together and is tremendously successful with an annual attendance of over 10,000.

I am sure that Dr. Konstantin Frank is looking down on us from above with a big smile on his face seeing the Finger Lakes Wine Region renaissance. Dr. Frank pioneered the introduction of the noble European wine grapes in the Eastern United States that are necessary to produce world-class wines. He met considerable resistance from both the university establishment and neighboring wineries.

In the last 10 years the tide has changed, and many Finger Lakes Region wineries are now offering wines made from the *Vitis vinifera* species of grapes. This shift from *Vitis labrusca* and French-American hybrid grapes to the European varieties has resulted in the production of many world-class wines. Through the cooperation of the wineries and joint marketing of the Finger Lakes Region, many more visitors will be influenced to visit the region.

Author's Note

As an amateur winemaker for 27 years and a vineyardist for 25 years, I share Fred Frank's optimism about the Finger Lakes Wine Region. Future trends involving the region include:

• An increased emphasis on red wine, reflected by more vineyard plantings of Cabernet Franc, Pinot Noir, Merlot, and Cabernet Sauvignon. The Finger Lakes Region used to be principally known for white wine and blends.

• A elevated willingness to grow new varieties, e.g., Sangiovese from Italy and Viognier from France.

• An upswing in interest in wines from the Finger Lakes Region in New York City, a large, sophisticated wine market. New Yorkers have become aware of the wine renaissance underway in the Finger Lakes Region that was triggered by the shift to *Vitis vinifera* grapes.

• Participation in the international trend to recognize the nutritional value of wine, including carbohydrates and vitamins—particularly vitamin B. Nutrients are present in varying proportion in wine depending upon climate and soil of the vineyard, grape variety, grape maturity at harvest, aging, etc.

• Increased recognition of resveratrol's value, particularly in red wine, both as an antioxident and in reducing the risk of cardiovascular disease. Wine's role—one or two glasses a day—in reducing stress has been widely noted.

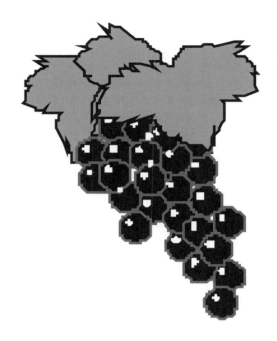

Glossary of Grape and Wine Terms

"When they [wines] were good they pleased my senses, cheered my spirits, improved my moral and intellectual powers, besides enabling me to confer the same benefits on other people."

George Saintsbury, *Notes on a Cellar Book*, Preface, 1920.

Acid—The natural fruit acid in grapes, e.g. tartaric acid.

Aftertaste—The sensation produced in the mouth and nasal passages after the wine has been swallowed.

Aging—The process by which wine develops character, mellowness, and smoothness.

Alcohol—Sugar is converted into alcohol and carbon dioxide by the fermentation process. Alcohol usually ranges from nine to 14 percent of the total volume in naturally fermented wine.

Amelioration—Adding water to grape juice to lower acid level.

Aroma—The component of the fragrance of wine that originates from the grapes used.

Astringency—The quality in wine that causes the mouth to pucker. The level of astringency is dependent upon the amount of tannin absorbed into the juice from seeds and skins. Astringency usually lessens with age.

Avinac—A fruit-flavored cordial.

Balance—A state in which acid, alcohol, fruit, sugar, and tannins are in harmony; none dominate the finished product.

Barrel Fermented—Fermentation in oak barrels instead of large stainless-steel tanks, imparting complex flavors and making the wine more full-bodied.

Berry—An individual grape.

Bloom—The blush on grapes that sometimes has the appearance of powder. It contains natural yeast.

Body—The feel of the wine in the mouth; described as light-bodied, medium-bodied, or full-bodied.

Botrytis Cinerea—A mold known as "pourriture noble" ("noble rot") sucks moisture out of grapes on the vine, concentrates sugars, reduces acids, contributes flavor elements, and, depending on weather conditions, usually improves wine quality. Botrytised grapes are used to make French Sauternes.

Bouquet—The component of the fragrance of the wine that originates from the aging of the wine.

Breathe—Wine is allowed to breathe by uncorking it a period of time before it is served to allow any undesirable odors to escape.

Brix or Balling—A scale indicating the percentage of sugar in the grape juice before fermentation that is an indicator of the alcoholic content of the finished wine.

Brut—An indication of the dryness of champagne. From sweet to dry, champagne is categorized as extra dry, brut, or naturel.

Bulk Process or Charmat Process—A method of producing inexpensive sparkling wine in vats or tanks instead of in the bottle.

Carbon Dioxide—The gas generated during the fermentation process. It is also generated in making champagne by the fermentation-in-the-bottle process or *méthode champenoise*.

Carbonic Maceration—The method of producing nouveau wines in Beaujolais that makes wine with a distinctive fragrance and taste. Whole grapes are placed in a container filled with carbon dioxide and allowed to stand for a week or more while the grapes are softened by natural enzymes. Fermentation begins from natural yeasts on the skins. The grapes are pressed, and the wine is fermented dry. Malolactic fermentation usually follows immediately.

Character—Used to describe a wine that possesses the bouquet, color, and taste of a quality wine.

Clos—French word for an enclosed vineyard.

Cluster-thinning—The process of trimming excess clusters from the vine to create fewer and larger grape clusters. It is also a technique used to prevent vines from overbearing.

Cold Duck—a sparkling wine, usually with a *Vitis labrusca* taste, is made in the United States and Canada by blending red and white wines.

Cold Stabilization—Chilling wine to 30° to 40° to precipitate out potassium bitartrate from the fermenting wine.

Corked or Corky—An unpleasant smell and taste caused by a bad cork.

Cream of tartar—The white crystalline deposit resulting from cold stabilization of fermenting wine. It is also called potassium bitartrate.

Cru—French word for growth. A type of classification that refers to specific vineyards of quality.

Cuvée—A blend of wine prepared for the production of champagne.

Decant—To pour wine carefully from a bottle in which sediment has been deposited into a decanter or carafe to prepare the wine for serving.

Delicate—Used to describe a wine, usually a white wine, with a light, subtle flavor. The fragile flavor can be overwhelmed by full-flavored food.

Dry—The opposite of sweet; that is, lacking in sugar. A dry wine is one in which all of the fermentable sugars have been consumed by the fermentation process.

Enologist—Winemaker.

Enology—The science of winemaking from harvesting the grapes to bottling the wine.

Enophile—One who appreciates wine. A lover of wine.

Estate Bottled—Indicates that the wine was produced and bottled on the property on which the grapes were grown.

Fermentation—The anaerobic (oxygen-free) process by which sugar in the presence of an active yeast is broken down into alcohol and carbon dioxide.

Fermentation Lock—A device filled with water that allows the carbon dioxide generated during the fermentation process to escape while preventing air (and therefore oxygen) from entering the wine.

Filtering—The process of clarifying wine by using filters.

Fining—The process of clarifying wine with a fining agent, e.g. Bentonite, during the winemaking process.

Finish—Flavors that remain in the mouth after swallowing wine.

Flowery—A word used to describe a wine with a bouquet that smells of fruit blossoms.

Fortified Wine—Wine to which brandy had been added to raise the alcohol content above 18 percent, e.g. Madeira, Marsala, Port, and Sherry.

Free-run Juice—Grape juice that flows from the press before pressure is applied. It is considered to be of higher quality than juice obtained after pressure is applied.

Fruit Wine—Wine made from fruit other than grapes, e.g. apples, apricots, blackberries, boysenberries, cherries, cranberries, peaches, pears, raspberries, or strawberries.

Generic Wine—A wine with definite type characteristics, frequently associated with a geographic area. Examples are Burgundy, Champagne, Port, Rhine Wine, and Sherry.

Grappa—A pomace brandy made in Italy. It is called marc in France.

Herbaceous—Herb flavor in wine such as Sauvignon Blanc and Maréchal Foch as well as other varieties.

Hybrid—A grape variety created by crossing two or more species, such as French-American hybrids developed by crossing European *(Vitis vinifera)* varieties with native-American varieties, e.g. *Vitis labrusca* or *Vitis riparia*.

Hydrometer—A device used in measuring the density of liquids. It is used to determine the Brix or Balling, the percent of sugar, of juice or wine.

Late Harvest—Grapes picked very ripe or overripe when they have a high concentration of sugar.

Lees—Sediment generated by the fermentation process that precipitates to the bottom of the carboy or tank.

Legs—The rills or rivulets of wine that flow down the side of the wine glass after swirling the wine. Legs are an indication of body.

Malic Acid—Malic acid contributes to the tartness of grapes and wine. It is second in importance to tartaric acid in the "total acidity" of must and wine.

Malolactic Fermentation—A secondary fermentation that converts harsher malic acid into softer lactic acid in the finished wine. It usually increases wine complexity but reduces fruitiness. It can reduce the total acidity of the wine by as much as one third.

Mead—Honey wine, occasionally blended with fruit wine.

Mellow—A term used to describe a soft wine, e.g. Merlot.

Meritage Wine—Wine made from grape varieties used in Bordeaux wine, e.g. Cabernet Sauvignon, Cabernet Franc, Merlot, Malbec.

Méthode Champenoise—The process of making champagne in which the secondary fermentation that produces the bubbles occurs within the bottle.

Microclimate—The climate surrounding the vineyards. It

could be influenced by the topology of the land or nearby bodies of water that have a moderating influence on the temperature.

Must—Unfermented grape juice with pulp.

Nose—The way a wine smells. A term used to describe the aroma of the grape and the bouquet of the wine. Wine having a pleasant aroma and bouquet is said to have a good nose.

Oak Aging—The quality of some wine, e.g. full-bodied red wine and white wine such as Chardonnay, is improved by the extract and tannin added by aging in oak barrels. European oak is usually from France, Austria, or Yugoslavia. Most French oak is from Limousin or Nevers. American oak, which imparts less extract and tannin than European oak, is grown in eastern United States as far west as Texas.

Oxidation—A change in wine, usually an undesirable change, due to contact with air. Oxidized white wine appears brownish.

Pedicels—Grapes are attached to the stem of their cluster by pedicels, through which they receive nourishment from the vine.

Perfume—The bouquet of wine.

Petioles—The thin stems between the grape leaves and the grapevine.

pH—The level of a wine's acidity. The desirable pH range for dry table wine is 3.2 to 3.6. If acidity is higher, the wine will taste harsh or green.

Phylloxera—An insect that attacks the soft, fleshy roots of the *Vitis vinifera* grape varieties. In the 19th century, thousands of European vineyards were destroyed by this root louse. By grafting European vines onto the hardy, resistant rootstock of native-American grapes, European vineyards were successfully replanted, reviving the wine economy.

Pomace—The residue, seeds and skins, from the pressing process.

Potassium Bitartrate (cream of tartar)—a salt of tartaric acid that precipitates as crystals in the fermenter or bottle, lowering the wine's acidity.

Press—Equipment that applies pressure to harvested grapes to force out juice.

Primary Fermentation—The initial, violent fermentation during which about two-thirds of the sugar in the must is converted into alcohol by the yeast.

Racking—Transferring the fermenting juice from one container to another. When using small containers, it is done with a syphon.

Reserve—Indicates wines that the winery considers special. Also called Private Reserve, Proprietor's Reserve, and Special Reserve. The term is not regulated.

Residual Sugar—The sugar level in the wine after fermentation is complete.

Resveratrol—A antioxident that occurs naturally in grapes to protect them against fungal infections. Its high concentration in grape skin reduces the risk of cardiovascular disease.

Riddling—The process of rotating bottles of ferment-in-the-bottle champagne a one-fourth, one-sixth, or one-eighth turn to move the sediment into the neck of the bottle so that it can be disgorged.

Secondary Fermentation—The slower, anaerobic (oxygen-free) fermentation that reduces sugar left after primary fermentation to alcohol.

Sediment—The solid particles deposited in the bottom of a bottle during aging, particularly in red wine.

Sensory Qualities of Wine—Clarity, color, odor, and taste are determined by winemaking practices, such as racking, addition of sulfur dioxide, fining, cold stabilizing, filtering, etc.

Sommelier—French for "wine steward." The individual in charge of wine service from the cellar to the dining room.

Sorbic Acid—Sorbic acid or its potassium salt is used in the fermentation of some sweet wines to deter yeast growth.

Still Wine—Non-sparkling table wine.

Sulfites—The presence of sulfur dioxide must be noted on the label; some people are allergic to it. Sulfites are used to preserve freshness in fruit and vegetables. Also, they are a natural byproduct of the fermentation process.

Sur Lies—Wine aged sur lies is kept in contact with the dead yeast cells and other sediment after fermentation has been completed. The practice has become common in making Chardonnay and is occasionally used for Sauvignon Blanc. The intent with sur lies aging is that a complex quality, a roasted-grain and toasty character, will be added to the wine.

Table Wine—White, pink, or red wine that is naturally fermented. It is usually consumed with food. It contains from seven to 14 percent alcohol.

Tannin—A substance present in grape stems, skins, and seeds. It promotes a clean, healthy fermentation, aids in stabilizing the color of red wine, and adds astringency to wine. Tannin contributes to the "body" of wine.

Tartaric Acid—The major grape acid. Tartaric acid and its salts usually provide over half the total acidity of musts and wines.

Teinturier—A grape variety used in a blend to add color to the wine.

Toasty—Sometimes used to describe the bouquet and taste of wine aged in oak.

Total Phenols—Phenols in wine include red pigments, tannins (the most important phenol), and similar substances.

Varietal Wine—A wine named for the principal grape variety from which it is made. It has the characteristic flavor and aroma of the grape variety for which it is named.

Véraison—The French word for the turning point in the vine's growth in early August when the green bunches begin to change color and ripen. The grapes have attained almost full size and most of their natural fruit acidity.

Viniculture—The process of grape growing, winemaking, and marketing wine.

Viticulture—Grapegrowing.

Vinification—The process of converting juice into wine by fermentation.

Vintage—The year in which the grapes were harvested and fermentation was begun.

Vintner—A wine merchant.

Wine Thief—A device used to obtain a wine sample for tasting or testing from a carboy, barrel, or vat. It is usually a glass tube open at both ends with a bulb at one end.

BIBLIOGRAPHY

Adams, Leon D. *The Wines of America*. Boston: Houghton Mifflin, 1973.

Allen, H. Warner. *A History of Wine*. London: Faber and Faber, 1961.

Amerine, M. A., and A. J. Winkler. *California Wine Grapes*. Bulletin 794. Agricultural Experiment Station, University of California at Davis, 1963.

Amerine, M.A. and V. L. Singleton. *Wine, an Introduction,* 2nd., Berkeley: U of California P, 1977.

Cattrell, Hudson and Lee Stauffer Miller. *The Wines of the East, 3 vols.* (*The Hybrids,* 1978; *The Vinifera,* 1979; *Native American Grapes,* 1980). Lancaster, PA: L & H Photojournalism.

Cox, Jeff. *From Vines to Wines*. Pownal, VT: Storey Books, 1999.

Galet, Pierre. *A Practical Ampelography*. Ithaca: Cornell UP, 1979.

Hedrick, U. P. *The Grapes of New York*. Albany: State of New York, 1908.

Jackisch, Philip. *Modern Winemaking*. Ithaca: Cornell UP, 1985.

Johnson, Hugh. *Pocket Encyclopedia of Wine*. New York: Simon & Schuster, 1998.

Klees, Emerson C. *Persons, Places, and Things In the Finger Lakes Region: The Heart of New York State*. Rochester: Friends of the Finger Lakes Publishing, 2000.

Lamb, Richard B. and Ernest G. Mittleberger. *In Celebration of Wine and Life*. San Francisco: The Wine Appreciation Guild, 1980.

Lichine, Alexis, et. al. *New Encyclopedia of Wines and Spirits*. New York: Alfred A. Knopf, 1974.

Morton, Lucie T. *Winegrowing in Eastern America: An Illustrated Guide to Viticulture East of the Rockies*. Ithaca: Cornell UP, 1985.

Ordish, George. *The Great Wine Blight*. London: J. M. Dent, 1972.

Patton, Dick. *Life With Wine: A Practical Guide to the Basics*. San Diego: Richard J. Patton Communication, 1995.

Reisch, B. I., et. al. "Melody Grape." *New York's Food and Life Sciences Bulletin 112*. Geneva, NY, 1985.

—. "Traminette Grape." *New York's Food and Life Sciences*

Bulletin 149. Geneva, NY, 1996.

Robinson, Jancis. *Guide to Wine Grapes*. New York: Oxford UP, 1996.

Schoonmaker, Frank. *Encyclopedia of Wine*. New York: Hastings House, 1973.

Taylor, Walter S., and Richard P. Vine. *Home Winemaker's Handbook*. New York: Harper & Row, 1968.

Vine, Richard P. *Commercial Winemaking: Processing and Controls*. Westport, CT: AVI, 1981.

Wagner, Philip M. *Grapes Into Wine: The Art of Winemaking In America*. New York: Alfred A. Knopf, 1976.

—. *A Wine-Grower's Guide*. New York: Alfred A. Knopf, 1973.

Winkler, A. J. *General Viticulture*. Berkeley: California UP, 1962.

INDEX